The Rebecca Code

ROMMEL'S SPY IN NORTH AFRICA AND OPERATION KONDOR

MARK SIMMONS

Mark Simmons was born in Plymouth, Devon, in 1953, into a family with a long tradition of service in the Royal Navy and Royal Marines. In the 1970s he served in the Royal Marines with 40 Commando RM, 3 Commando Brigade, and with the Commando Logistics Regiment.

Mark has written over 100 articles for publications in the UK and USA, primarily on naval/military and travel subjects. He is a correspondent for *Warships International Fleet Review* magazine, and runs an internet bookshop, Rowan Oak Books, selling a wide range of titles.

His other books include: *A Crack in Time* (2004), a search for the echoes of the Am̶ ̶ ̶ ̶ ̶ ̶ ̶ ̶ *nt and the Cross* (20 ̶ ̶ ̶ ̶ ̶ ̶ ̶ ̶ ̶ ̶ ̶ ̶ ̶ ̶ World War; and *Th̶*

Firs

Spe
The
The
Stro
ww

© N

The right of Mark Simmons to be identified as the Author
of this work has been asserted in accordance with the
Copyrights, Designs and Patents Act 1988.

British Library Cataloguing in Publication Data.
A catalogue record for this book is available from the British Library.

ISBN 978 0 7524 6870 9

Typesetting and origination by The History Press
Printed in Great Britain
Manufacturing managed by Jellyfish Print Solutions Ltd

Contents

Acknowledgements

Like many people my interest in the German use of the Rebecca Code during the Abwehr Operation *Kondor*, began with reading Michael Ondaatje's 1992 Booker Prize winning novel *The English Patient*. I was further inspired by the late Anthony Minghella's 1996 Oscar winning film of the same name. Much is to be admired in both, at the heart of which is a love story between the desert explorer Count László Almásy and the English woman Katherine Clifton.

Most readers I trust will be familiar with the book and/or the film of *The English Patient*, so there is no need to relate it here, other than to say much of the background of the Western Desert and Cairo was the setting for real events. Also the character of Almásy depicted in book and film is a marked distortion of the real man, and his end was in real life very different. Many of the other characters in the real story are discounted, no doubt for good reason in that fictional account.

The English Patient was not the first attempt in fiction to tell this story. The first book to cover the *Kondor* mission was by war correspondent Leonard Mosley in his 1958 publication *The Cat and the Mice*. Mosley was in Cairo at the time the events took place and he interviewed the German spies John Eppler and Peter Monkaster (Heinrich Gerd Sandstette) in prison. He also kept in touch with Eppler after the war. However in view of the later accounts, one written by Eppler, and later firm evidence, it is certain that Eppler strung him along to a degree in order to embellish his own image as some sort of James Bond. The 1960 film *Foxhole in Cairo* was based on Mosley's book, the film poster calling it 'the greatest spy story of the desert war'. That is true, but the film has little else to recommend it. In the film James Robertson Justice plays the British intelligence officer, a naval commander, tasked with catching the spies, and Michael Caine is seen in one of his early roles as a German W/T operator.

Other writers also used the bones of the *Kondor* story in fiction, Ken Follett in *The Key to Rebecca* (1980) which was filmed in 1989, and Ken Deighton in *City of Gold* (1992). Both books relied heavily on personal accounts. Also Anwar Sadat's *Revolt on the Nile* (1957),

A.W. Sansom's *I Spied Spies* (1965) and John Eppler's *Rommel Ruft Cairo* (1960) published in English as *Operation Condor Rommel's Spy* (1977). It is doubtful if they would have used Almásy's *Rommel Senegenal Libyaban* (1943), translated into English by Gabriel Francis Horchler as *With Rommel's Army in Libya* (2001). Or for that matter come across Almásy's diary of Operation *Salam*, held by the Imperial War Museum in the Lloyd Own Papers.

The Secret MI6 files were closed in 2003 and released to the public in 2006. It was my aim, therefore, to bring the four eyewitness accounts by Almásy, Eppler, Mosley and Sansom together with the official files and tell the true story of the Rebecca Code and Operation *Kondor.*

Secondary sources that have been useful include Hans-Otto Behrendt, *Rommel's Intelligence in the Desert Campaign* (1980). John Bierman's *The Secret Life of László Almásy* (2004), Paul Carell's *The Foxes of the Desert* (1958), Christer Jorgensen's *Hitler's Espionage Machine* (2004) and Saul Kelly's *The Lost Oasis* (2002).

I am grateful to the staff at Bletchley Park, the Imperial War Museum, the Intelligence Corps Museum, the Public Records Office, Royal Geographical Society, AKG Images, Hunt Library, US National Archives, Hungarian Geographic Museum, Bookends of Fowey, and the Forest Park Hotel Cyprus.

I am also hugely indebted to the following people: Shaun Barrington my Editor at The History Press for his enthusiastic support for this project right from the start. Group Captain L.E. (Robbie) Robins AEDL, another enthusiastic supporter, for free use of his extensive library, his hospitality, and for reading an early draft making many excellent comments and suggestions. My late Aunt Olive Hard for her illustrations of Egypt during the war years. To Ann Willmore, book dealer at her shop Bookends of Fowey and an expert on the work of Daphne du Maurier, who supplied a wealth of information on the publishing history of the novel *Rebecca*.

Finally my wife Margaret as always gave her whole hearted support in the nuts and bolts of building a book, with proof reading, index building etc. Thanks to all.

Glossary

Abwehr	German Secret Service meaning 'defence' in German
Auto-Saharan	Italian Long Range Desert Patrols
BRSS	British Radio Security Service
'C'	Head of British Secret Intelligence Service MI6
CFSO	Chief Field Security Officer
DSO	Defence Security Officer
Enigma	German code machine system
FSP	Field Security Police
GC & CS	Government Code and Cypher school, Bletchley Park
Golden Square	Pro-Axis group of Iraqi officers
Grand Mufti	Muslim religious/political leader
Horchzug	radio monitoring platoon, later company Afrika Korps
KG 200	Luftwaffe special unit
LRDG	Long Range Desert Group (British)
MI5	Military Intelligence Section 5, British counter-intelligence service
MI6	Military Intelligence Section 6, British espionage service, often known as SIS
MI8	Military Intelligence Section 8, British War Office (Army) cryptanalytic service
MI9	Military Intelligence Section 9, Escape and Evasion
Muslim Brotherhood	Egyptian Nationalist Organisation
ND	*Geheime Nachrichtendienst* (German Security Intelligence Service)
NKVD	*Narodny Kommissariat Vnutrennich Dyel* (Soviet Secret Police)
OKH	*Oberkommando der Heeres* (German Army High Command)

OKW	*Oberkommando der Wehrmacht* (German Armed Forces High Command)
Pasha	high official of the Ottoman Empire, used as title
Pianist	Abwehr slang for clandestine radio operator
RTR	Royal Tank Regiment
RSS	Radio Security Service
SAS	Special Air Service (British)
SD	*Sicherheitsdienst* (SS Secret Service)
SDF	Sudan Defence Force
Siguranza	Romanian Security Police
SIM	*Servizio Informazione Militaire* (Italian Secret Service)
SIME	Security Intelligence Middle East (British)
SIS	Secret Intelligence Service (British) otherwise MI6
SOE	Special Operations Executive
Turpitz Ufer	HQ Abwehr Berlin
ULTRA	Ultra decodes decryption of encrypted Axis radio communications classified Ultra Secret
W/T	wireless telegraphy
Y-Section	radio-reconnaissance and listening posts, British and German

Prologue

Troodos Mountains, Cyprus, September 1936

It was not someone 'Sammy' Sansom expected to come across on the descent from Mount Olympus in a small Ford saloon. A young fair-skinned woman was being sick beside the road. She was sat on a fallen pine tree, in the shade of the trees, her head between her knees unaware of the car's approach. Or not caring.

Sansom had to stop. Here was a lady in distress, a European. But more important to him it was the right action to take.

'Excuse me Miss, can I help?' Sansom climbed out of the car and brushed off his clothes although there was no need. He was a dapper man.

'Oh dear' she said looking up at him, 'I must look a sight.' Her eyes were startlingly clear blue. She shook her dark hair away from her face. She noted the lightweight suit and knew instantly the type, a colonial been here for years. 'I'm not a Miss, but Mrs Browning.'

'Are you ill Mrs Browning?'

'No, other than being pregnant and suffering morning sickness. Perhaps I was foolish to try to walk to Mount Olympus.'

'In this heat, which is deceptive in the mountains even early in the morning, maybe it was not wise. Where are you staying Mrs Browning?'

'The Forest Park hotel.'[1]

'Yes I know it, near Platres, would you care for a ride back to the hotel? I am Alfred Sansom, but call me Sammy, insurance salesman for the Gresham Life Assurance Society from the Egypt office.'[2]

'That would be kind Mr Sansom; I doubt this is going to pass quickly. It really is tiresome, something you men are lucky not to suffer.' He was strikingly handsome, with the fashionable moustache that all men seemed lost without. And his eyes were dark pools, inscrutable but his smile was friendly and not condescending.

Sansom nodded and waited until Mrs Browning got up in case she felt faint. Her slim angular face was pale but she was steady on her feet, and strode with purpose to the car. She caught him by surprise with her height and speed of her walk, but he reached the passenger car door in time to open it for her.

'A reader I see Mr Sansom' she said, picking up the book Sansom had left on the passenger seat. 'My goodness' she said reading the title, 'how strange, *The Loving Spirit,* one of mine.'

'You are Daphne Du Maurier?'

'That's my maiden name.' She opened the book to the page marked by a scrap of neatly folded paper and read: 'Chapter fourteen. For five years Joseph Coombe was an inmate of the Sudmin Asylum.'[3] 'What do you think Mr Sansom? It's not often I meet a reader.'

'I like it; it inspires me to visit Cornwall one day.'

'Oh do, how I wish I was there now. Mind you,' she added quickly 'I find Cyprus invigorating away from the heat and multitudes of Alexandria, my husband's in the army there.'

She handed Sansom the book and climbed in. It was only a short drive to Platres and the hotel. The air fresh with the scent of pine and cypress trees was cooling which did much to restore her. By the time Sansom opened the door for her the colour had returned to her face.

'Would you like me to dedicate the book Mr Sansom?'

'That would be kind.' He retrieved the book for her and handed her a pen from his briefcase. 'Sign it to Sammy please.'

Sansom smiled at the dedication on the title page and read. 'To my saviour Sammy in Cyprus, Daphne Du Maurier.' He closed the book. 'Thank you. Are you working on another book Mrs Browning?'

'Yes Sammy, another Cornish novel about a great house, haunted by the dead wife of the owner. I will call her Rebecca.'

'Good I will look forward to that.' Sansom gave her a slight bow, climbed into the car and drove away.

Inscrutable she thought, but she did not understand the British, the Empire builders that is, who could live out here, probably only ever going home to school as a child. Yet he had been a godsend that morning.

Sansom was 26 and Daphne was 29 that day.*

*The pregnant Daphne du Maurier did stay on the island of Cyprus in 1936, writing her novel *Rebecca* published by Gollancz in 1938. There is no evidence she met Alfred Sansom. This is fiction; however everything that follows did happen.

Part I

THE CHARACTERS

1. Johannes Eppler, Beirut, May 1937

SPRING WAS A GOOD TIME to be in Beirut before the heat in July and August became oppressive on account of the excessive humidity, driving people inland to seek the more agreeable conditions of the mountains.[1]

Johannes Eppler was 23 in May 1937 when he went ashore from the luxury of the *Khedive Ismail* passenger ship that had brought him from Alexandria to Beirut. He had travelled on the ship many times, which sailed between Piraeus, Famagusta Cyprus, Beirut and Alexandria. Eppler was small, on the thin side, with a square, handsome face, small moustache and blue eyes, unusual amongst Egyptians but not unknown, even going back to the time of the Pharaohs. He looked what he was, a young wealthy Egyptian, play-boy/man-about-town.[2]

His Egyptian name was Hussein Gaafar but his parentage was German. His mother had inherited a small hotel in Alexandria to which the family moved and she managed. His father died soon afterward and his mother later married the wealthy Egyptian lawyer Salah Gaafar who adopted her son. Johannes becoming Hussein Gaafar, holding joint nationality. He became fluent in Arabic, German and English, the latter learnt while attending English-speaking schools in Alexandria and Heliopolis. He was baptised Roman Catholic; his mother had come from the Catholic south of Germany. As a young man he also made the pilgrimage to Mecca.

The German embassy in Cairo had contacted him, acting on orders from the Abwehr headquarters in Berlin, to find likely people with German connections abroad. This clandestine meeting seemed melodramatic to Eppler. He was to meet a Herr Haller, a stranger who would have a half page, number 145, of Juliette Adams' book *L'Angleterre en Egypte,* to match the half given to Eppler. They would meet at the Saint George Hotel where he would stay.[3]

He arrived the day before the meeting and that night picked up a woman, a Hungarian, Ilona, in the hotel. The bars and dance floor of the Saint George were often buzzing with all sorts of people of many nationalities. He spent the night in her arms in his room.

Eppler rose early on 15 May for a swim; he hoped Ilona would be gone by the time he returned. The meeting with Haller was not until the evening. He swam out into the bay from the diving jetty of the Saint George. Swimming was an exercise he was fond of having been brought up in Alexandria where trips to the beach and swimming were part of daily life. He swam far out for perhaps a mile into the sea. A fast motor launch passed nearby, swamping him with its wash. He surfaced, choking, to see a pretty blonde girl waving at him from the stern. He did not take it as an ill omen; he was looking forward to the clandestine meeting.[4]

Returning to the hotel there was little to do but wait. He had a whisky and soda down on the bar terrace. He had never been a devout Muslim and he enjoyed alcohol. He found Islam to be radical, like the desert extremes of hot and cold. Not suited to his free spirit.[5]

After a siesta in his room, at about 8.00pm he began to dress for the meeting. At 8:20pm the reception desk phoned to inform him someone was waiting to see him.

Soon there was a knock on the door. Opening it Eppler saw a tall, fair, blue-eyed man. Smiling he presented his half page and said 'Haller.' The two half pages fitted. Eppler was not impressed. Was Haller trying to unsettle him? And how could they send such an obviously northern European man for a secret meeting in the Middle East?

They went down to the bar and found a secluded corner. Both ordered whisky.

'You know,' began Haller, 'that we don't think it's of any importance for you to do two years of military service with the army proper.'[6]

Eppler was glad to hear this but did not interrupt.

'It is for this reason that the Attaché in Cairo arranged this meeting. We have other things in mind for you.'

Eppler, irritated, informed Herr Haller he did not like people arranging his life, but was open to suggestions.

It made little difference to Haller who continued with what seemed to be a prepared speech. 'Since you are German and born in 1914, you must serve your two years with the forces. That is a decree of the Führer's which you must obey, like anybody else. But we are reasonable people, we are prepared to talk, especially in the case of Germans living abroad, like yourself, and there are always possibilities.'

Eppler began to feel bored and wished Haller would get to the point. He was hungry, so took Haller into the big hotel restaurant where he had reserved a table. There he showed Haller his Egyptian passport. Haller was surprised by the number of stamps and visas.

'When I am in Germany from time to time, I have found it useful to have my German passport with me, otherwise it is more convenient to use this one.' Eppler explained that he had found the authorities suspicious in Germany.

'No need to be offensive.'

'It is only an observation, no judgement.' Eppler found Haller's manner insolent, but stayed silent. It was them that wanted him; after all they had paid for all this. And he felt hopeful it might help in his quest for adventure. He waited for Haller to show his hand.

Haller continued. 'I need hardly tell you that we are fully informed about you, down to the smallest detail. We know precisely with whom we are dealing.' He then concentrated on the wine, finding the 1931 Chateau latour Bellegarde first class.

Eppler was uneasy; he later wrote that he found Haller to be 'aggressively Aryan' and did not like the 'supercilious bastard'. If he had to deal with Herr Haller very much his Abwehr career would never get off the ground.

'My colleague Rohde will be here in a quarter of an hour,' said Haller.

'This Rohde, would he be your chief?'

Haller acknowledged this, and that Rohde was responsible for the Middle East.

The meeting took a turn for the better with the arrival of Rohde. He was of medium height and build, and was tanned after many years in the east, well-dressed with impeccable manners. A man from the old Germany. Straightaway he began to chat in an informal, engaging manner. Haller however remained silent for most of the rest of the evening, much to Eppler's relief.

'It would be a waste of time,' said Rohde, coming to the point, 'to make a little speech about the Fatherland, a sense of duty and service to the people. I really can't expect you to feel such things. The gap between you and the new Germany is too great. You live in a different world.'

Eppler agreed eagerly that 'philosophising' with him was pointless, but said that he was keen on 'anything that smacks of adventure'.

Rohde continued, outlining the nature of the work of a secret agent. They needed information about the military of other countries, but as a Military Attaché in Greece and Turkey, his own freedom of movement was limited.

Thus he needed 'trusted men who were at home in the Levant.' He felt Eppler fitted their requirements. But he warned him that Secret Service work was 'no picnic' and was 'dangerous', requiring great courage and intelligence. The agent was on his own most of the time. He wanted relations between them to be clear from the start, and should they fail to reach an agreement they would go their separate ways as if nothing had happened.

Eppler liked his frankness and felt he could work with this man. He told him he was not acting out of patriotism and that he felt more Egyptian than German; they were lucky that Egypt was basically a British colony and he wanted to see the back of the British. Rohde pointed out that Egypt had been independent since 1922, but admitted that the British had certain 'privileges'. Eppler agreed this was the case but that Egyptian independence was a sham, conditional on guaranteeing lines of communication to the British Empire. The British also had 'suzerainty of the Sudan' as well.

'Otherwise, Herr Rohde, we are quite independent.' Rather, in fact, Egypt was just Britain's 'Lancashire cotton plantation'. Certainly Egypt's plight would affect his decision. He pointed out he would not be bought; money was of no consideration.

Rohde advised Eppler to sleep on it and they would have a more private meeting the next day. And now they should 'enjoy themselves' with the cabaret. There was an interesting belly dancer gyrating in the spotlight on the dance floor that they should investigate. They agreed to meet at the Hotel Metropole where Rohde was staying – without Herr Haller – the next day.

The next morning after his swim Eppler rang Rohde, changing the meeting place to his room at the Saint George. The Metropole was known to be 'German' and watched by the French Secret Service. Rohde agreed. At their second meeting Eppler accepted the German's proposal. An appointment was made to meet again, in July in Athens, where he could sign on with the Abwehr.

During the intervening weeks between the meetings in Beirut and Athens, Eppler returned home to Alexandria. In June 1937 the city was still very cosmopolitan with large Greek and Italian populations. He did not waste time and arranged a meeting with the leader of the Muslim Brotherhood. He himself was a fringe member of the Brotherhood. Odd given his playboy lifestyle and the wealthy pro-British background of his adopted family but he felt new ideas were overdue and would take off in Egypt; he wanted to be part of it. The Brotherhood's aim was to rid the country of foreign rule. More important for Eppler, he knew it had a secret intelligence branch. He was already thinking how he might help his potential new masters. Could he instigate contact between the Brotherhood and the Abwehr, and would it be useful to the Brotherhood? He needed a meeting with its leader, Hassan el Banna.

A distant cousin and member of the Brotherhood's inner circle took him along to meet Banna at the Mosque of el-Khalid Ibrahim. Eppler found Banna more like an old Turk; he was a fanatic and 'fanatics were dangerous'.[7] In private, Eppler asked his questions but Banna did not answer for a while, looking him straight in the eye almost unblinking. When he did speak, it was slowly. He told Eppler that he was not the first to ask such questions. The Italians were putting feelers out; Mussolini had become the self-appointed 'Protector of Islam'. They were trying to infiltrate Egyptian Nationalist organisations.

Eppler interrupted the flow. 'At the moment, I am not trying to do anything, Hassen bey, nothing at all. No one has sent me.'

'Good. We are first and foremost an Arab and a religious movement.' Banna pointed out that he was willing to use the Europeans of all types for his own aims; however he could not compromise on the supremacy of Islam in Egypt, which the Europeans were against, be they British, Italian or German. But he was not against contact if Eppler could provide it.

It struck Eppler after this meeting that he had reached a crossroads: either he worked for the Abwehr and kept the meeting with Rohde, or went back to his old lifestyle. However, he did not want merely to become a German lackey. He kept making contacts, the next being the 'Greenshirts', Egyptian Nationalists. The organisation had grown out of a disaffection with the Anglo-Egyptian Treaty, and was extremely anti-British. He vaguely knew its leader, Ahmed Hussein, who months before had sought his advice on a trip to a Nuremberg Nazi Party rally. He did not like the man but was willing to cultivate him.

In the coffee houses of Alexandria he found out that Ahmed Hussein was in Tanta. The city was 80 miles southeast of Alexandria, the centre of the cotton ginning industry and the rail hub of the Nile Delta region. It was an ideal opportunity to try out his new Lancia sports car on a long run. The journey proved to be frustrating at times, as he weaved through the slow traffic of donkeys, camels and carts that were in no hurry to make way for the speeding car, even when he used the horn.

Hussein was at prayer in the Sheikh Said el-Badawi mosque. Reluctantly Eppler joined the prayers but felt 'I would rather have a decent meal than spend time in prayer.' Then he spoke with Hussein who agreed to help Eppler if he could.

Eppler did not stop there but went on to cultivate other nationalists, particularly in the Egyptian Army, where many of the young officers were 'fellow travellers'. One who was trying to organise a cell was Hussein Sabri Zulfikar. Eppler flew down to Cairo to see him. Like many wealthy young Egyptians, Eppler had learnt to fly on a Tiger Moth at a British-run flying club.

He met Zulfikar at the army officers' club in Zamalek for a game of squash, and to sound him out about how things stood in the army. He already knew many officers sympathised with the Brotherhood, but would they act? After the game they found a coffee house where Eppler asked Zulfikar whether he would be willing to help him, which he warned could be risky. Zulfikar agreed instantly.

During this busy time Eppler got married, revealing the impulsive side of his nature. Sonia was a Danish national with a touring ballet from Copenhagen. Eppler first saw her in a nightclub. 'I shall never forget her entrance. She was stunningly beautiful, with hair the colours Titian loved to paint, dark red with glints of gold.'[8]

After two weeks they were married at the Danish Consulate in Cairo on 25 June, much to the vexation of his stepfather, Salah Gaafar. He called Sonia 'the acrobat' and refused to see her. He informed his stepson, 'You'll have to manage on what you get.' While he made no increase to his allowance however, he did not cut him off.

Thus, unwittingly, the pro-British Salah Gaafar helped push Eppler toward the Germans, although really his impulsive stepson needed little encouragement.

Sonia had to stay with the Danish ballet company but agreed to meet her husband in Athens once the tour was over. Provided Eppler was taken on by the Abwehr they would travel on to the World's Fair in Paris and then visit Denmark, before he went on alone to Berlin.

2. Eppler, Athens and Berlin, July–August 1937

Eppler arrived in Athens on 20 July 1937, a Tuesday. He obeyed his instructions to telephone Rohde when he arrived, doing so from the luxurious King George Palace Hotel, a fairly new establishment with an uninterrupted view of the Acropolis. A meeting was arranged and Eppler met Rohde's driver in the hotel lobby. After a short drive Rohde greeted him at the door of a large villa 'that could just as well have been in Munich, if it had not been for the Acropolis visible over the roof.'[1]

Rohde took him to the study, which overlooked 'the sundrenched garden'; the room was 'tastefully furnished' and 'immaculately clean'. The building was quiet and appeared deserted, the only sound being the faint murmur of traffic noise from the road.

After brief pleasantries Rohde went over the offer he had made Eppler in Beirut.

'So that there can be no misunderstandings. You know I prefer to work without complications. If you have any doubts left, please tell me frankly.' Eppler did have questions but did not interrupt, instead lighting a cigarette. The air was soon thick with Turkish tobacco smoke as both men smoked.

Rohde told him he would have to go to Germany for training, and on his return Rohde himself would be Eppler's boss. In time he might work for others or on his own.

'We've thought it over, you realise. I am only a link in the chain, and it has been decided to establish you firmly in the Middle East. After your training period has ended, that is where you will begin your work, provided of course the political situation remains what it is today.'

His cover was first class, his job was 'exclusively' to collect military intelligence. He was to keep out of politics. 'We are soldiers, not politicians.'

Eppler told him he had recently got married; Rohde knew already. He admitted he was surprised. It would have been better if Eppler was not married, as with any agent, but it changed little. They would give Sonia a monthly allowance, an amount to be decided in Berlin. Eppler of course would be paid, and have expenses; the latter would be decided by Rohde once Eppler was in the field, and they could be generous.

Eppler told Rohde of the groundwork he had begun in Egypt. He was pleased with this; it was something he could build on later. Eppler emphasised that he would not work against the interests of Egypt or Denmark, Sonia's country. They went on to discuss pay, which would start at 1500 marks a month. Eppler also asked for a contract.

'You will have to discuss that in Berlin. They'll fall about with laughter when you tell them; they'll never have heard of anything like that.' However the two men did reach an agreement after more bargaining. Eppler found Rohde 'obstinate but not unreasonable'.

Later they went out for lunch to the Alex restaurant, at the Third Reich's expense. The Alex served Egyptian and Greek cuisine and Eppler found the food good. He felt reassured to be dealing with someone with such obvious good taste.

After a leisurely lunch they returned to the villa where once again Rohde did most of the talking. Eppler was sure someone was listening in on their conversation, perhaps even noting every word that was said, but he was not concerned. Rohde told him about the course he would attend in Germany, which would give him 'the final polish for this profession, hard work is the only way. Without the technical skills acquired during the training period, no agent can get by these days.'

He told Eppler to trust no one – even within his own department, because it was an organisation riven by 'jealousy', a dangerous enemy. 'Trust no man, use him, but never trust him, or he will let you down.' Eppler found this somewhat alarming. But the attraction to remain was overwhelming. Especially when he heard Rohde's next words.

'The name of your most dangerous adversary is the British Secret Intelligence Service. Its various departments and missions will be something you'll have to spend a lot of time over during your training course.' Rhode explained that it was more than likely that Eppler's first enemy contact would be with British Naval Intelligence. Their Section South 3 covered the Levant, Arabia and Persia. MI6 would be the field operatives. 'They are tenacious, these boys, once they have picked up the trail, they will not give up the chase.' He suggested the best course was 'not to draw attention to yourself'.

The most valuable aspect of the espionage course would be the acquisition of technical skills. 'These things will be of the greatest possible value to you.' Rohde also told Eppler to put maximum effort into the military training course. 'Take it seriously and go through with it.' By the end he would be fully trained and have 'everything a good agent needs'.[2]

On the day the Epplers were due to leave Athens they both met Rohde for lunch at the Alex, at his invitation. They spent three hours there before Sonia went off to do some shopping. Meanwhile Rohde took Eppler to his house to give him his final instructions concerning where and when to report to Abwehr headquarters.

On 15 August, Eppler arrived at 76/78 Tirpitz Ufer, named after Grand Admiral Alfred Von Tirpitz, on the Bendlerstrasse, the home of the Abwehr. It had rained early that morning but the sun had dried the roads and pavements, although the day remained cloudy. He felt Paris was certainly more alluring and more fun but Berlin was 'an attractive and friendly city'.[3]

The Abwehr HQ (Abwehr meaning 'defence') was a four-storey building, part of the Bendler block that also housed the Reich Navy offices; it overlooked the Landwehr Canal, brown and languid. It reminded Eppler of a 'low court', a 'depressing' building. At the entrance the commissionaire took his name and made a call, told him he was expected and directed him into the bowels of the building. The quarters were cramped, with small offices and a dark corridor, for the HQ was made up of two town houses.[4]

A smart young lieutenant conducted the initial interview, checking Eppler's details. Then he was handed on to a Major Maurer from Section 1 Secret Intelligence. Within hours he started training, studying large scale maps of the Middle East.

Training in earnest took place in the River Havel area, 40 miles west of Berlin at the Wehrmacht Special Training School of Quenzgut near Lake Quenzsee. Eppler was placed with Helmut Mutze, a man of about his own age, who would stay with him throughout his training and report on his progress.

Eppler was put through his paces for two weeks in hot and humid weather, which he did not altogether appreciate. He was either soaking wet or sweating 'like a pig' and every bone in his body ached. He seemed to have to crawl or run everywhere.

He learnt about the use of explosives and how to use them against railways and bridges. Much time was spent on the rifle ranges with a variety of weapons. Parachute training he found difficult. 'I was frightened out of my life by being thrown off a 5m high board into a pile of sawdust and then bullied through a series of ground exercises. Forward rolls, backward rolls; a whole afternoon of nothing but somersaults – how I got to hate somersaults.' He came to loathe his parachute instructor, Sergeant Schafer, who called him a sack of potatoes, always qualified with a barked 'Sir.' Schafer had a roly-poly frame, more sack-like than Eppler, but was able to touch the ground 'as softly as a feather', making Eppler green with envy.

He was sure that his companion Mutze was reporting on his progress – or lack of progress – all the time, that he was some sort of minder. They went out together socially and eventually Mutze admitted his role. 'At each stage of your training I am supposed to make out a report of your aptitude, both physical and psychological. I must describe your general attitude, official as well as private, your relations with the opposite sex and your ability to hold your liquor.'

Eppler told Mutze he could put in his report, that he, Eppler, had had enough of parachute jumping and blowing things up; 'I am no anarchist, let them blow things up. I was told all I needed was a rough idea, and I've got that now.' Mutze told him not to worry, to calm down; he would soon be back in the Middle East and more than likely working under Rohde, who held him in high regard.

Shortly afterwards they both left for Striegau in Lower Silesia, East Prussia, and the Abwehr training school not far from the Gross-Rosen concentration camp. Here Eppler was schooled in the mysteries of coding and decoding, ciphers and radio work. It was a two-week concentrated course, but Eppler still managed to get into the city of Breslau for some recreation.

In his account written after the war Eppler had little to say about the Germany he visited in 1937, although it was of course undergoing massive upheaval. Breslau, capital of Silesia, was a city with a large Nazi faction; in the 1932 election the party had received almost half the city's popular vote. Jewish persecution was well under way; the city once had a large Jewish community, the sixth largest in the country. The small Polish community was also being persecuted, and one could be arrested for speaking Polish in public.[5]

After a month of training, Eppler was ordered back to Berlin. An interview with Admiral Canaris, head of the Abwehr, was scheduled.

★★★

Wilhelm Franz Canaris was 50 in 1937. He was born in the small mining town of Aplerbeck near Dortmund Westphalia, the son of the wealthy industrialist Carl Canaris. In his youth Wilhelm convinced himself he was related to the Greek Admiral and freedom fighter Constantine Kanaris. This is said to have influenced his desire to join the navy, but it brought him into direct conflict with his father, who told him if he wished to join the armed forces, which was not a family tradition, he would join the cavalry and a commission was sought in a Bavarian Regiment. Fate intervened, his father dying of a stroke in 1904. Canaris' mother, Auguste, allowed her son to choose his own future. He passed his high school exams with high marks, and due to his linguistic skills – he spoke three languages – he sailed through the entrance exam for the navy. He joined the Imperial Navy Academy on 1 April 1905, where a military infantry course was followed by nine months of naval training. A fellow cadet found him 'slow to speak but quick to listen'. He was tough but displayed a good sense of humour.[6]

By the time of the First World War, Canaris was serving in the South Atlantic on the light cruiser SMS *Dresden* as an intelligence officer. He had already gained a reputation for being reliable and competent. The *Dresden* had been part of Admiral Maximilian Graf Von Spee's squadron that had sunk the British Pacific Fleet at Coronel, the first defeat for the Royal Navy in over a century, with the loss of two armoured cruisers and nearly 1600 men. For three months the Germans had been masters of the South Pacific but too late, with British forces closing in, decided to run for home via the South Atlantic. The Admiralty had despatched a powerful fleet under Admiral Frederick Charles Doveton Sturdee, which caught up with Spee's force off the Falkland Islands. On 8 December 1914 the powerful battle cruisers *Inflexible* and *Invincible* trapped the German force and sent them to the bottom of the Atlantic.

Only the *Dresden* survived the Battle of the Falklands owing to her superior speed. For several months she played a game of hide-and-seek with the British fleet, much to the chagrin of the Admiralty in London. Canaris was instrumental in arranging clandestine meetings with supply ships. However, the *Dresden* was finally cornered near Chile by HMS *Glasgow,* which opened fire although both ships were in neutral waters. Here Canaris showed his guile and a degree of courage by going over to the British ship – which was still firing although a white flag had been raised – to parley. Meanwhile his colleagues opened the sea cocks and lay charges to scuttle the ship, which blew up while Canaris was still on board the *Glasgow.*

In Chile the crew of the *Dresden* faced internment for the rest of the war. But Canaris got to the capital Santiago and managed to obtain a Chilean passport from the German Embassy in the name of Reed Rosas. By Christmas, having crossed the Andes by donkey and foot, and having contracted malaria, he reached Buenos Aires. Taking some time to recover with the help of the local German community, he finally took the Dutch steamer *Frisia* back to Europe.

While on board the *Frisia* he got on well with the English passengers, and became a popular player at the bridge tables. The ship's first port of call was Plymouth, but no suspicion had been cast on Senor Rosas. Canaris disembarked at Rotterdam and from there, still using his Chilean passport, he crossed the border into Germany.[7]

These exploits made Canaris's name within the Imperial German Navy. His name would also have been familiar to Commander Mansfield Cumming, 'C' of MI6, and maybe even brought to the attention of Winston Churchill at the Admiralty for the first time.

Back in Berlin he was awarded the Knights Cross in September 1915. It was then he joined the ND (*Geheime Nachrichtendienst*) the Security Intelligence Service.[8] Early the next year he was sent to Madrid, an ideal appointment with his perfect Spanish, his job being to provide accurate intelligence on Allied shipping movements. Again he used his pseudonym of the Chilean Senor Reed Rosas; he took a flat not far from the German Embassy, a place he never visited as it was constantly watched by Allied agents. Canaris soon organised resupply for U-boats in the Bay of Cadiz using Spanish ships. These ships – often commissioned by Reed Rosas for use in South American waters – would undertake extensive trials around the Iberian Peninsula, where under the cover of darkness they would rendezvous with German submarines. Thus Canaris had a direct effect on the war at sea. British Intelligence in Spain observed: 'The situation with German U-boats is especially serious. They do what they want in the Mediterranean.'

The British SIS (Secret Intelligence Service) became aware of a new German agent in Spain and sent their own man, the young Scot Stewart Menzies, to eliminate him. But Menzies, a future head of SIS, could not find Canaris, who left Spain on 21 February 1917. It was during his first period in Spain that he met a young Spanish Army officer, Francisco Franco, who was as enigmatic as Canaris himself.

Suffering from recurring malaria, and still using his Chilean passport, Canaris headed for Germany overland. However, he was arrested by Italian police at Genoa, who had been tipped off by French Intelligence that Reed Rosas was a German spy, information gained from a source within the German Embassy in Madrid that had heard the name there.

Canaris, obviously ill and claiming that he was merely travelling to a Swiss clinic, talked himself out of jail. But the border guards at Domodossola were not so easily fooled and removed him from the train on which he was travelling, locking him up again. He was arrested with a priest and his subsequent release may have been facilitated by Vatican pressure.[9]

He was put onto a ship bound for Marseilles, where the Italians hoped that the French authorities would deal with the Chilean-German, whoever he was. Luckily the ship's captain was Spanish and it seems Canaris bribed him not to put in at Marseilles. Instead he was put ashore at Cartagena, still feverish with malaria. By the middle of March he was back in Madrid, where he applied for active service.

The head of German Naval Intelligence in Madrid, Hans Von Krohn, told Canaris he would have to remain in Spain for the time being. He spent six months building up more contacts. However, he did not know that his spy ring had been compromised by Room 40 British Naval Intelligence in London that had broken most of the German ciphers. The importance of naval matters in Spain meant the country came under the NID (Naval Intelligence Division) rather than the British SIS.[10]

Canaris finally left Spain in October 1917, picked up by U-35 off Cartagena. He reached the Austrian base of Cattaro on the 9th. His skill in Spain was rewarded with the order of the Iron Cross first class; part of the citation noted 'the extraordinary skill with which he had carried out his mission'.[11]

Canaris then joined the submarine service in Kiel. It was there he met Erika Waag, the woman he would marry after the war. He was posted to Pola, joining U-*34*, which took a toll of British merchant-men in the Mediterranean.

The entry of the US into the war tipped the strategic balance decisively against Germany. In October 1918 all U-boats in the Mediterranean were ordered home. By this time Canaris had risen to command U-*128*. He reached Kiel on 8 November to find the ships of the High Seas Fleet gripped by revolution and mutiny and flying red flags. Three days later the war ended, as did the world Canaris had been brought up in.

The navy he loved suffered a complete breakdown of discipline. Yet the officer corps soon rallied, undermining communist attempts to control the navy. Canaris, although no longer a field agent, was quick to act during the communist attempt to take over Germany 1918–21, aiding the assassins of the communist leaders Rosa Luxemborg and Karl Liebknecht. The German communist threat finally ended after the failure of the uprising in 1923.

In the 1920s Canaris's linguistic skills were well used on trips to Japan, Spain and Sweden, where weapons and ships were secretly purchased for the German Navy, ignoring the terms of the Treaty of Versailles.

In January 1921 the German military intelligence service was officially reborn as the Abwehr; but it was a tiny organisation, a shadow of its former self with only a handful of officers and some clerical staff at HQ. By 1933 its chief was a naval officer, Captain Conrad Patzig, who reluctantly took the appointment, which army officers looked down on as a dead-end job. Thus by default the Abwehr came under the remit of the navy, which was good for both services.[12]

It was Grand Admiral Erich Raeder, head of the Kriegsmarine – who wanted to keep the Abwehr in the navy's control and knew Patzig did not have the heart for the job – who finally decided on the then Captain Wilhelm Franz Canaris for the job. Although Raeder was not overly fond of Canaris he knew his reputation and skill with intelligence work. Canaris accepted with enthusiasm and sped across country to take up his new appointment on 1 January 1935.

Patzig had hated the job; showing Canaris around HQ he asked him if he knew what he was getting into, especially with the Nazis. 'I'm an incurable optimist. And as far as these fellows are concerned, I think I know how to get along with them.' In fact Canaris was involved in two plots to depose Hitler in 1938 and 1939, and kept MI6 informed of the dangers the Nazis posed before the Munich Agreement. He may even have met with 'C' – Sir Stewart Menzies – when he was in Spain in December 1942 at Algeciras, with peace terms in mind should Hitler fall. Menzies, who seldom ever left London, spent a few days in nearby Algiers and Gibraltar at the same time as Canaris was at Algeciras. Patrick Reilly, Menzies' personal assistant, was given leave at the time and stated that 'I am inclined to the view that he gave me leave at that time because he wanted me out of the way while he was abroad.' Reilly did not learn of Menzies' absence from his desk until 40 years later.[13]

★★★

In September 1937 Eppler arrived back at the Abwehr HQ for his interview with Canaris; the offices at Tirpitz Ufer were known to be watched by foreign agents. Major Maurer (whom Eppler had met before his training) took him to the Admiral's office, which was small, with a desk and a filing cabinet. Later it would boast a signed portrait of General Franco and a painting of a Japanese demon, a present from Japan's ambassador to Berlin, Baron Oshima.[14]

Eppler described Canaris as small like himself; he seemed 'tired and withdrawn'. His speech was slow, but he was not unfriendly. Eppler was most struck by his blue eyes. He had heard the story of Canaris's Greek origins, but he did not look Greek to him.[15] In fact it was about this time that Canaris found out his family was of Italian origin. He was given an elaborate family tree by Cesare Ame, head of the SIM (Italian Military Intelligence Service). The family had moved from northern Italy to Germany in the seventeenth century.[16]

It is obvious that Eppler took a dislike to Canaris. He thought him a 'cynic' and felt he could not trust him, describing him as 'devious' and a 'hater'. According to Eppler he was not allowed to address Canaris, but could only answer his questions. Perhaps given that this was his first meeting with the Admiral, he may have been overly influenced by others' views of Canaris.

The Admiral asked him many questions; he particularly wanted to know about Rohde. He advised Eppler to stick with his German name and to forget Gaafar and his Arab background.

'You know they don't like that sort of thing at the top. They would say you are tainted with the Semitic brush.' Eppler had to sign a form declaring his Aryan origins.

'They tell me you got top marks in your course. Well done! And give my regards to Rohde. He knows his business. I like him.'

'Herr Rohde will be pleased to hear that sir,' said Eppler.[17]

***

At Sagan near Frankfort-Oder, Eppler went on to complete his training with the army, what he later called a 'hero-factory'. Here he joined the Tank Corps at the Hindenburg barracks, becoming Private Eppler. One sergeant-major told him he was lucky to be there: 'We'll make a tough man of you here. Like Krupp steel, that's how hard you'll be when you leave us.'

He spent one whole morning learning how to salute. Latrine duty was particularly stimulating 'scrubbing the thunder boxes'. De did however also gain useful skills, such as handling the Spandau 7.92mm 42 machine gun, the 'Hitler violin'. He completed five weeks' training and returned to Berlin. There he confided to Major Maurer his disappointment in not getting to grips with a tank.[18]

Eppler had a few weeks' leave with Sonia in Copenhagen before returning to the Mediterranean to meet Rohde in Athens. According to Eppler, he was briefed on his first mission on a trip to Cape Sounion, 'where we sat under the columns on the broken steps. The air was clean and smelt of seaweed.' Was this his romantic side distorting the facts? The Temple of Poseidon hardly seemed the place for a briefing. His mission was to find the Mufti of Jerusalem who had moved to the Lebanon, away from the British. The Germans wanted to talk with the 'Grand Mufti' Hadji Mohammed Amin el Husseini.[19]

3. László Almásy

A HUNGARIAN EXPLORER AND AVIATOR, László Almásy's life story was to become the stuff of books and films. A tall and slender man, he had a large, curved nose giving him a bird-like appearance, although he had an engaging, shy smile. He was also a chain smoker, seldom seen without a cigarette. He first learned to fly in England, when he was sent to a small private school in Eastbourne at 17 Carew Road run by Mr Daniel Wheeler; at fifteen he was a hopeless student. Even the redoubtable Mr Wheeler, MA, FRGS, could not improve his academic abilities. However Almásy did join the fledgling Eastbourne Flying Club where he obtained his first pilot's licence aged seventeen. Motoring was another of his passions, and in November 1913 he was fined for 'driving a motor car at a dangerous speed' in Eastbourne.[1]

At the start of the First World War Almásy returned home and with his brother Janos joined the 11th Hussars Regiment. He fought against the Serbs and Russians, and after a period of leave in 1916 he transferred to the Austro-Hungarian Air Force and took to the air against the Italians. In one engagement his aircraft was badly shot up and he was wounded, but managed to get the aircraft back before crash landing on friendly soil. After recovering from his wounds he spent the last months of the conflict as a flight instructor.

At the end of the war Hungary lost much of her territory and came under a revolutionary communist regime. Almásy took up arms in a counter revolution with nationalist forces ousting the communists, during which thousands of pro-communists were massacred in Budapest.

In the early 1920s Almásy came to the attention of Steyr Automobile, an Austrian company founded by Hans Ledwinka in 1915. They offered him a job, inviting him to go to Africa to establish their brand name in the lucrative Egyptian market; while in their employment Almásy won several car races using Steyr vehicles. It was while in Egypt in 1926, during a drive to the Sudan, that Almásy became interested in the desert. In 1932 he took part in the expedition to find the legendary lost oasis of Zerzura – 'The Oasis of the Birds' – with three Britons, Sir Robert Clayton-East-Clayton, Squadron leader Hugh Penderel and Patrick Clayton. The expedition used cars and an aeroplane, cataloguing prehistoric rock art sites such as the 'cave of the swimmers' in Uweinat and the Gilf Kebir, both already well known to the Bedouin Arabs and attributed to the *djinn* (unpredictable spirits). The Bedouin gave Almásy the nickname *Abu Romia* (Father of the Sands).

In 1932 Sir Robert Clayton-East-Clayton died in England, almost certainly from an infection picked up during the exhausting search for the Zerzura. His wife Dorothy, an accomplished pilot in her own right, went to Egypt after his death, determined to locate the Zerzura and complete his work. The 1933 expedition to the western edge of the Gilf escarpment was led by Patrick Clayton, who would later help form the British Long Range Desert Group during the Second World War.

It is said that Lady Dorothy did not like Almásy, she would not even shake hands with him; Patrick's wife Ellie felt the same and 'simply couldn't stand him'. Dorothy thought him untrustworthy and both women were aware of the Cairo gossip concerning his fondness for young men, although he also had a reputation as a womaniser, probably created as a smokescreen. John Bierman in his account of Almásy's life states that he was bisexual rather than homosexual, but whatever the truth, given the attitudes of the time it is perhaps not surprising that these women shunned him.[2] Later that year, Dorothy, having returned to England, died in a mysterious plane crash at Brooklands Aero Club, close to the motor racing circuit in Surrey. Although the coroner returned the verdict of 'death by misadventure', some eyewitnesses believe she could have landed the plane but instead flung herself from the cockpit and that she had committed suicide.

Almásy went on to explore the area of the Gilf Kebir plateau and the Egyptian Sand Sea up until 1936. The expeditions were often funded by the wealthy Egyptian Prince Kemal ed Din, a desert explorer in his own right, who had written about the Gilf Kebir for *National Geographic* in 1921.[3]

On 1 September 1939 Germany invaded Poland; two days later Britain and France declared war. For Almásy there could hardly have been a worse scenario. He had seen it coming and knew that his country, Hungary, was likely to ally itself with Germany. It is said

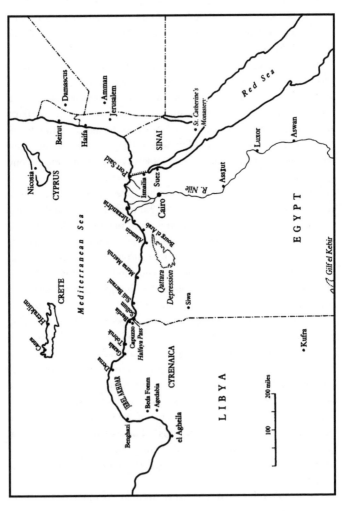

The Middle East, Libya, Egypt and the Eastern Mediterranean.

that Almásy approached Sir Thomas Russell Pasha, Chief of the Cairo Police – a tall, handsome and cultured man who loved Egypt and hunting in the desert – offering his services as a desert adviser and guide to the British Army.[4] His offer, if it was ever made, was turned down. Almásy was advised to leave Egypt or risk internment. The British thought he was an Italian spy, while the Italians thought he was a British spy. This confusion may have come about because of his willingness to work as a surveyor for whichever colonial power paid the most. He was often strapped for cash.

It appears he left Cairo, flying himself, on 22 July 1939. Back home he became a reserve lieutenant and flight instructor with the Royal Hungarian Air Force. He came to the attention of the German Abwehr when his book *The Unknown Sahara,* first published in 1934, was released in a German edition in 1939. It landed on the desk of Major Franz Seubert, head of North African affairs, and while the Germans considered North Africa and the Mediterranean mainly an Italian concern, Seubert was recruiting useful people with Middle Eastern knowledge. He put it to his colleague, Luftwaffe Major Nickolaus Ritter (who had responsibility for the Balkans) that he might like to sound Almásy out the next time he was in Budapest.

Ritter met Almásy in Budapest, at his ground floor flat, part of the Almásy family mansion on 29 Miklos Horthy Avenue.[5] He thought him 'a cavalier of the old school', but was generally impressed. During one visit Almásy revealed that he was on good terms with General Aziz el Masri, an Egyptian nationalist whom the British had had removed from his position as chief of staff of the army. It dawned on Ritter that Almásy might persuade El Masri to come over to them. They talked over plans to get the General out of Egypt and to Berlin, from where he might be able to foster rebellion within the Egyptian Army. Almásy felt it could be done; he was invited to Hamburg to discuss details and was seconded from the Hungarian Air Force to the Luftwaffe. There is no doubt Almásy was itching to get back to the desert and he would have overplayed his hand, a fact Ritter and Seubert were well aware of. However the plan remained at the back of Ritter's mind.[6]

It was not until February 1941, when the Germans arrived in North Africa, that Ritter's Commando within the 10th *Fliegerkorps* began to take shape, comprised of Abwehr men. Their role was initially to get General el Masri to Germany, but their secondary role was to get agents into Egypt, both of which would be aided by Almásy's skill as a pilot and desert explorer.[7]

Before Almásy left for North Africa, to work with the Germans, a friend asked him how he was able to accept working against the British, many of whom were his friends. He replied all would be within 'military honour'. But he also confided, 'The only thing that really interests me there is to dig out Combyses.' Rommel could supply the petrol to do so. He was referring to the lost Persian army of Combyses, which Almásy had been searching for in 1935. According to Herodotus, the 50,000-strong army had vanished in the desert over 2000 years ago, while marching from Thebes, via Kharga, to subdue the Kingdom of Siwa; but it never reached Siwa or returned to Egypt.[8]

4. Alfred Sansom

On Tuesday 11 June 1940 Alfred William Sansom applied to join the Field Security Branch of the Corps of the Military Police after seeing vacancies advertised at the Kasr el Nil barracks in Cairo. On the same day Mussolini declared war on the Allies and Italian aircraft bombed Malta. On the 18th Winston Churchill would make his 'Their finest hour' speech to a packed Houses of Parliament, still reeling from the evacuation of Dunkirk two weeks earlier.

Sansom was small, five feet five inches, always well turned out and wearing cologne. His portly figure was hardly the archetypal military policeman. He saw this himself: 'I scarcely had the stature for the job.' Given his trim moustache and the slim switch cane he often carried he was more akin to a young Hercule Poirot. He had much in common with Eppler; both men had spent much of their lives in Egypt, Sansom being born there. Both had European parents and were partly educated in Europe. The two cold, damp years Sansom had spent at a boarding school in England were enough for him. His father had wanted him to go to Cambridge but Alfred managed to persuade him to allow him to return to Cairo and study Arabic at Al-Azhar, the oldest Islamic university. Like Eppler, he was fluent in several languages including Greek, Italian, French and Arabic. He, too, could pass for a native and often did.

Sansom found filling out the MP application form to be tedious but given his previous 'trade' as an insurance salesman he was used to such things. The form as such made little difference as the three officers on the interview panel did not read it. Instead they left it on the table and proceeded to ask most of the questions he had answered on the form. His lack of height made no difference, and anyway the Field Security Branch was soon transferred to the Intelligence Corps. He was quickly commissioned and sent to the Kasr el Nil barracks for training.[1] For most of the garrison troops of Cairo, home was the citadel of Muhammad Ali, a large complex of training grounds, sports facilities and married quarters, The Kasr el Nil barracks on the banks of the Nile were much smaller, able to cater for about 1000 men. They had a renowned hardy variety of bedbugs, proof against any insecticide.[2]

Sansom completed his courses in Intelligence and Field Security, military administration and discipline in three weeks. Promoted to full lieutenant with his own section, he was sent to the Western Desert, 'where my duties were understandably limited to checking passes, intercepting tins of bully beef on their way to the black market and supervising the burning of secret documents in homemade incinerators.'

The desert war had hardly begun when Sansom found himself at Mersa Matruh on the Mediterranean coast. Only a few hours from Cairo, he found the desert at night eerily quiet and majestic. 'The moon was up, a full one, and the scene was all beauty and peace. The sand-dunes reflected strange shadows, and the sea gleamed like steel.' However the peace was soon shattered by an air raid in which his batman, Jones, was hit by flying shrapnel from a bomb that Sansom felt whizz past him. He grabbed his tin hat and flung himself to the ground. When he got up minutes later he found Jones lying on the ground with a 'gaping chest wound'. Nothing else was damaged in the tent apart from Jones, who had taken the full force of the blast. Jones had made no sound, 'not even a moan, although he might have been in great pain.' Sansom found his first-aid training inadequate to deal with such a serious wound but he managed to stop himself panicking and put some blankets over Jones to keep him warm, recalling something about shock and the cold. Jones was still conscious and was even apologetic not to have got 'the tent in order – and I was looking forward to this expedition.' Sansom gave him a tot of whisky and rushed off to find the MO, whom he almost dragged to the scene. The doctor told him to get a grip or he would be his next patient. The doctor gave Jones a shot of morphine, and told him he would soon be alright. Jones knew better, asking Sansom to make sure his mother got his camera, which had been her parting gift. 'All I could do was nod,' recalled Sansom. 'The MO went on reassuring Jones until he died.' This incident had a profound effect on Sansom, giving him a fatalist view of life, that he was 'living on borrowed time'. It also made him callous 'and sometimes apparently braver than it was in my character to be.'[3]

In the early months of the desert war Sansom's duties included chasing Bedouin, who would pilfer anything they could from camps, including documents left unattended. He was also tasked with making weekly reports on the morale of the troops, which he found generally high. Only in the Egyptian Army did he find cause for concern, if not alarm.

> The morale of the Egyptian troops is at the lowest possible ebb. It was unlikely to rise unless we are defeated in battle, in which event they would almost certainly go over to the enemy. If Mersa Matruh is attacked they will not resist, but will probably help the attackers. Our position would be stronger without them even if no replacements are available.[4]

The small army waited for the Italian attack, knowing their defences to be insufficient. They faced the real prospect of Egypt being invaded. In September 1940 the former Egyptian Prime Minister Ismail Sidki wrote an article in the newspaper *El Ahram*; 'The Italian offensive is not an aggression against Egypt, but against another belligerent on the territory of a third occupied power.' The average Egyptian looked forward to an Axis victory merely to get rid of the British, without considering the full implications. Meanwhile Sansom was occupied in tracing arms stolen from the Egyptian Army that had been supplied by the British and were finding their way into subversive elements of various nationalist groups.

Early in September the Italians began their offensive with a spectacular artillery barrage on Musaid, which they rapidly occupied, also taking the airfield and empty barracks at Sollum after another bombardment. A movement against the Halfaya pass ran into stiff British resistance. After four days they reached Sidi Barrani and Sofafi, some 70 miles from Mersa Matruh. Marshal Rodolfo Graziani was in no hurry to get there; he wanted a better road laid and a water pipeline to the frontier. German officers visiting the front felt the Marshal would not move unless Mussolini gave a definite order, so there would be no resumption of the advance for months.

Sansom felt his 'best contribution would be to reduce the liaison with the Egyptian Desert Army to a minimum', but he continued to visit Prince Ismail Daoud for weekly morale reports on the force. Prince Daoud, a member of the Royal House, commanded the Egyptian desert force in style. His command post was a large and luxurious marquee, and his meals were brought in from Alexandria.

Sansom 'thoroughly enjoyed staying for lunch or dinner', although he was well aware that the rank and file 'lived on an appalling diet of dried beans and lentil soup, with an occasional bit of meat, and regarded the officers with envious hatred and were ready to fire the first shots into their backs.'[5] The British soldiers felt relief when the news came that the Egyptian Army was to be withdrawn from the desert on Churchill's orders. The Egyptian soldiers were equally delighted to get away from roughing it in the desert and back to the bright lights of Cairo.

During the final months of 1940 Sansom's time was largely taken up with checking the Bedouin crossing the desert, which after all was their land. They were willing to work for any of the trespassers if they were paid. Before the soldiers and armies of the infidels came, they had been the Western Desert's only inhabitants, taking no notice of frontiers as they followed their goat herds. For the British, the most reliable agents were those who criss-crossed Libya, which the Italians were occupying.

The Bedouin were first used as spies by the Italians. According to Sansom, 'Our side had underestimated them as an intelligence nuisance because they seemed unlikely spy material; but experience showed that with good briefing and at very little cost they could pick up titbits of information that were cumulatively quite valuable to a trained intelligence officer.' Even if they only reported troop movements and vehicles they saw 'they were well worth their very small pay.'[6]

Major Gerry Baird was the chief DSO (Defence Security Officer) at Mersa Matruh. A detention camp for suspects had been built and was soon full, but only Baird and Sansom could speak Arabic so they had to spend hours interrogating Bedouin suspects. Some of the Bedouin played a risky double game. 'There was nothing remarkable about that. Having no loyalties, many of the Bedouin took money from both sides.'

It was about three months after the Italians had taken Sidi Barrani, by which time Sansom had been promoted Captain, when he went down with sand fly fever and was evacuated to the General Hospital at Helmieh on the outskirts of Cairo. A debilitating disease transmitted by the bite of an infected sand fly, its symptoms include headaches, fever, red eyes, tiredness, nausea and pain in the back and joints. By the time Sansom was discharged from hospital the military situation had changed and the Italians were in full retreat. General Sir Richard O'Connor's Western Desert Force directed by General Archibald Wavell had taken 38,000 Italian prisoners at Beda Fomm, along with 1000 vehicles, 73 tanks and 237 guns, and was advancing toward the Libyan frontier.[7]

Sansom did not return to the desert but was appointed Chief Field Security Officer for Cairo. It was only just over six months since he had applied to join the Intelligence Service.

Part II

THE SCENE

5. Cairo, Spring 1941

SITTING AT HIS DESK IN GHQ Cairo, 'Sammy' Sansom felt disappointed to be back in the city. He was away from the action in the desert, where Wavell's and O'Connor's troops had chased the Italians over the border. Tobruk had fallen in January and after Beda Fomm in February the Italian 10th Army had virtually ceased to exist. It looked like the war would be over for Egypt, and he 'did not fancy the idea of taking root in another desk job.'[1]

However, on the morning of 12 February Lieutenant General Erwin Johannes Eugen Rommel had arrived at the Castel Benito airfield south of Tripoli, invigorating all who came into contact with him with his untiring enthusiasm. He was nearly 50, squat and powerfully built; his grey-blue eyes were usually friendly but could blaze with fury if he was provoked.[2] There would be more war to fight.

Sansom felt lucky to have Francis Astley 'Bones', a six-foot goodhumoured giant, as his second in command, who had been teaching at the University of Cairo when the war broke out. They had both joined Intelligence at the same time, responding to the same advertisement. While Sansom was drafted to the desert, Astley went to the Canal Zone. In Cairo they stayed together until the end of the war, which was unusual in the department, where officers changed frequently. By that time Astley had become Sir Francis Jacob Dudley Astley, sixth baronet, an inherited title he was not altogether happy with, due to the ribbing he got within the department. The title expired with him in 1994.

Military security had been in the hands of Astley when Sansom returned from hospital, a huge job that was overwhelming him. There were thousands of British and Commonwealth troops in and around Cairo, as well as Poles and Free French, all with different uniforms. Astley and Sansom decided to test security by dressing two intelligence officers in German uniforms, giving them orders to be 'conspicuous'. They were to make a list of all those who questioned them or attempted to arrest them. They wandered around Cairo for two days without any reaction before finally giving up.

Following a reorganisation Sansom largely left security of military installations to Astley. The army were housed in camps and barracks around the city, the British mostly at Heliopolis, Helwan held the South Africans, Mera the Indians and Maadi the New Zealanders. The majority lived under canvas, eight men to a tent in the hot and humid conditions. It was hardly healthy. No doubt the troops fresh from Britain found Cairo a culture shock, with its colour and unfamiliar smells of herbs and spices. There was an abundance of foods in the shops, yet poverty was everywhere; beggars were everywhere, crying for 'baggsies'. Peddlers and hawkers tried to sell them all sorts of goods from shaving brushes to dirty magazines. Prostitutes and pimps could be found on most streets. 'Hi, George! You want my sister, very clean? Good price for you.'

'Morals and morale don't mix'; so began one of Sansom's reports on morale of the troops.

> … the troops spirits depended mainly on the price, quality and especially availability of prostitutes. This was the natural result of separating young and fit men from their wives and girlfriends. In the desert, where women did not exist except as muffled shapeless Bedouin, sex was just a wry joke. It was no laughing matter in Cairo and Alexandria, with all that flaunting of the most powerful of aphrodisiacs, a pair of pretty legs.

He lamented the attempts by moralist pressure groups to kerb this. But he had to admit, 'Even after the bloodiest fighting there were always more brothel casualties than battle casualties in the service hospitals.'[3]

VD was a scourge of the troops, despite the efforts at sexual education by the medical officers. There were seven VD clinics attached to hospitals in the city, and with an average of 100,000 troops in Cairo in the years 1941–1942 they were busy. Some brothels were approved, but were pretty uninspiring places run by the RAMC; 'On the ground floor, sitting on his stool was the RAMC man doling out one French letter, one tin of ointment and one pamphlet to each supplicant.' In March 1941 the increase in VD coincided with the return of the 7th Armoured Division from Cyrenaica. In Cairo the oldest profession was in demand, centred on the seedy quarter of Clot Bey to the north of Ezbekieh Gardens. The main street was known as Berka.

Berka was officially out of bounds marked by signs, a black cross on a round white background, which applied to all ranks. By entering the area a squaddie risked trouble with the MPs, even arrest, but neither they, nor the risk of VD, seems to have dissuaded those troops looking for a good time. The Berka boomed until two Australians were murdered there in the summer of 1942, after which it was closed down, straight away halving the cases of VD.

It was frowned upon for officers to visit brothels, as it set a bad example to the men. If they contracted VD most would swear that they had picked it up in a private house. Many officers were less streetwise than the men and were more likely to be mugged or robbed, partly because they carried more money and valuables.

To the squaddies the Egyptians were 'Wogs', a slang term for a dark-skinned individual with distinctly racist connotations. It was soon attached to anything Egyptian, including 'Wog Beer' and 'Wog Grub'. With so many troops on the streets, many drunk and bored, fights and disturbances flared up frequently. Egyptians got no compensation when the soldiers damaged their property, brawling in their cafes and bars, and the locals were often robbed or attacked. The Egyptians apperently found the Australians the most loutish, although most nationalities could be rowdy.[4]

Freya Stark liked the vibrant city at this time.

> In and out of the official world was the Levantine society of Cairo dripping gems and substantially unchanged from the days when Thais wore Alexandria's most expensive togas. It would gather in the Muhammad Ali Club where fatherly waiters and huge chandeliers preserved their Victorian solidity, into which cheerful troops broke now and then and asked for drinks. Having got them from the shocked fifth-columnist head waiter, they would ask for women, and the police were sent for: as I left once I found my fat chauffeur with his head in his hands, rather bashed by a South African annoyed with him for not being a taxi.

> Beyond these quarters, the whole of Cairo itself buzzed like a hive, carrying from age to age, from foreigner to foreigner, from dynasty to dynasty, its blind traditions and long poverties. In these crowded quarters I came to have many committees-teachers, clerks, workmen or the lesser rank of government servant, living in small alleys up narrow stairs, hard lives not untouched by dreams.[5]

When on leave, many of the soldiers went to see the sights. Unsurprisingly the Pyramids were the greatest draw. A horse-drawn gharry would be hired in the late afternoon to avoid the heat, and from Gezira Island they would drive over the English Bridge and south along the Nile past the Foud I University to Giza. The climb to the top of the Great Pyramid took about half an hour. A couple of locals could be hired to help a weary soldier if necessary. In 1905 Elizabeth Cabot Kirkland made the climb and noted that 'The fatigue was great, the charges small. We had three Bedouin Arabs, one on each side and one behind. Many of the stones are four feet high and it would be impossible to climb them without this assistance.'[6] Having reached the top and admired the view the sightseers some-times carved their initials alongside those of Napoleon's troops. After descending many went to see the Sphinx, looking rather sorry behind the British-built blast wall, sandbags piled up to the 4000-year-old chin. Many then had their photograph taken sitting on a camel with the Pyramids in the background.

Daphne du Maurier disliked Egypt; during a visit in 1936 she found Cairo no more to her liking than Alexandria. She described the Pyramids as 'just like a couple of slag heaps' and swore never to go on any more foreign postings as an army wife. Her husband Fredrick 'Tommy' Browning also disliked the country.[7]

G.C. Norman, a desert soldier, described those Cairo days:

> Life at the base, 'the rigours of the Cairo campaign' as the English lan-guage newspaper cartoonist put it, gave us our first real taste of the totally unreal life which was being lived back there, while we were 'up the blue,' Cairo was a dream world of music, theatres and opera, cafes and cinemas, museums and mosques, where we strode the crowded, unblacked-out streets like conquerors, accepting the homage of shop keepers, dragomen and shoe-blacks as to the manor born.[8]

G.S. Fraser, a wartime clerk at GHQ, found Cairo had a voice of its own.

> Every street in Cairo has the character of Cairo, but hardly any street has the character of itself. Everything, every note that at first seems distinctive, is repeated again and again.

The tenement which is crumbling away at one side, like a rotted tooth; the native restaurant open to the night, from which there comes a soft clapping of palms on tables and a monotonous chanting; the maze of narrow streets that leads to a cul-de-sac, where a taxi has gone to die, the sudden green and red glitter of lights, glimpsed through a curtain from a cabaret; the sudden patch of green wasteland, the glimpse of the river, the white glitter of buildings on the other side, the curved mast of the feluccas, pulled down at the top as if by invisible strings; these things, and not things only, but people and incidents, are repeated, the baldish purple-looking ox that has collapsed in the gutter and is having its throat cut; the street accident with twenty shouting spectators in white galabeyas; the woman in black, sitting on the pavement, nursing her baby at a dusty breast; the legless beggar propelling himself forward, on a little wooden trolley, with frightful strength, with his hands. Unknown districts of Cairo, as I used to pass them on the crowded, clattering trams, would terrify me; so much suffering, unexplored, inarticulate life.[9]

As the city filled with troops, Sansom quickly developed a plain-clothes section for the civilian side of intelligence work. Although personnel could be interchanged easily, a section consisted largely of one officer, a warrant officer and ten NCOs. Soon Sansom had five sections in his department, but this was not even 100 men to cover security within the city. They used informers and spies, but there were few of these when Sansom first took up the reins, 'and some were of doubtful use and reliability', so he began to recruit more. There was no lack of volunteers; some were only interested in pay while others worked free of charge. 'We had to sift the good from the bad, reliable from unreliable, and especially the genuine from the double agent and the plant.' In this Sansom had a distinct advantage, not only because he knew the country and the people well, but because he had – through social contacts made before the war – unofficial as well as official means of checking credentials.

Thanks to this close screening I quickly learnt that almost all who volunteered their services were unsuitable for the work. On the other hand recruited agents were not so keen on proving themselves and their information on the whole proved more reliable.[10]

In March 1941 many in the Egyptian military, including Sansom, felt that the war was over for Egypt; however, things were about to change. On 22 February, ten days after Rommel arrived in Africa, Mr Anthony Eden, Foreign Secretary, Sir John Dill, Chief of the Imperial General Staff, General Wavell, Air Chief Marshal Longmore and Captain R.M. Dick RN (representing Admiral Andrew Cunningham) with their staffs, had secretly arrived in Greece by air. During meetings with the Greeks, Eden, with the full agreement of the Chiefs of Staff and the Commanders-in-Chief Cairo, told them that maximum help would be given to them as soon as possible, as Greece faced the prospect of German invasion.[11]

Some 100,000 men, many from the Western Desert Force, were committed to the campaigns in Greece and Crete. O'Connor's men were experienced and Wavell had to draw on them to form the core. But Greece and Crete were by no means the only campaigns the Middle East High Command had to deal with. By the time the Germans invaded Greece in April the British had lost part of Cyrenaica. Malta was under heavy air attack and there was also unrest in Iraq. Wavell had seen no option but to try and defend Greece although he lamented 'that this war was not "one damned thing after another" it was everything in all directions at once.'[12]

6. The Western Desert

THE AREA OVER WHICH THE Allied and Axis armies fought, the Western Desert, is one of the most arid and desolate regions on earth, covering some 1500 miles from the Nile Delta to Tunisia. The Egyptian part covers 250 miles from the Delta to the border with Libya and is 150 miles north to south at its widest point between the Mediterranean coast and the Oasis at Siwa. South of Siwa is the Egyptian Sand Sea and the Gilf Kebir plateau, the most inhospitable region. East of Siwa, running northeast, is the Salt Marsh of the Qattara Depression, which ends about 40 miles from the Mediterranean near a small railway station called El Alamein.

Thus the Western Desert had two open flanks, the sea to the north, and the desert to the south. It was the opportunities provided by these flanks that gave rise to specialist Allied troops: the Long Range Desert Group (LRDG), the Special Air Service (SAS) and the commando units. One unit of specialists that opposed them was the Brandenburgers, Ritter's Abwehr commando, which came under the umbrella of the German 800th Brandenburger Lehr Regiment. Almásy and Eppler served in this organisation.[1]

The desert is not consistently the flat, grey expanse dotted with scrub that it first appears. There is cover, for the desert rolls and moves, providing much 'dead ground', and there are long rocky ridges of limestone. The great coastal ridges, the escarpment, rises west of Mersa Matruh to a height of 450 feet, a steep blocking wall that vehicles can only cross via roads cut through the Halfaya Pass and Sidi Rezegh. The escarpment can also be crossed by camel as the Bedouin have done for centuries. During the Second World War some of the camel tracks were marked out with oil drums, like buoys marking a channel at sea.

The Bedouin were always there and ready to trade, but there was little other life in the desert in 1941. The greatest torment for the soldiers was the flies, droves of them from dawn to dusk. The blistering heat made the slightest movement draining; any cut or abrasion was soon infected by sand. Every man who fought in the desert suffered the constant chafing from fine sand in dirty clothing, which caused lesions or desert sores. If sand got under the foreskin the result was agonising; many men had to be circumcised.

The nights were freezing and tracks could be washed away by torrential rain. Sand storms, the scourging *Khamsin*, could come at any time or season.

> The Italians hated the desert, and kept it at bay by building stone houses in their camps, laying out paths and little gardens. The Germans fought it with science; their stores were full of foot powders, eye-lotions, insect repellents, mouth washes and disinfectants. The British, Australians and New Zealanders simply ignored the desert. They slept in blankets on the ground, and were not unduly worried about germs.[2]

There were few towns and those only on the coast. The desert provided a huge battleground for open mobile warfare only limited by supply. In his history of the Eighth Army Robin Neillands wrote: 'There is nothing to sustain an army here; every gallon of petrol, every drop of water, every round of ammunition, has to be carried in. The first point to keep in mind about the war in North Africa from 1940–43 is the chronic problem of supply.'[3] These precarious supply lines were vulnerable and were an ideal target for the Special Forces.

★★★

While Almásy was being wined and dined by the Abwehr in 1939, some of his British pre-war desert acquaintances, Ralph Bagnold, Pat Clayton, Kennedy Shaw and a new boy, Captain Rupert Harding-Newman, were setting up the Long Range Desert Group (LRDG). The story of this, the most successful of the 'private armies' that flourished in the desert war, began when two ships collided in the Mediterranean in October 1939. One limped into Port Said for repairs; on board was Major Bagnold of the Royal Corps of Signals en route to take up an appointment in East Africa. He decided to take a few days to look up old friends in Cairo and the buzz soon got around that he was in town, it was mentioned in the *Egyptian Gazette.*

Baggers, as he was affectionately known, went to see General Maitland (Jumbo) Wilson, commander of British forces in Egypt, and suggested forming 'a mechanised desert raiding force' but it was turned down. However Bagnold was sure of himself and not easily put off. He therefore went over Wilson's head and asked for an interview with General Archibald Wavell; within an hour of the request he was facing the Commander in Chief across his desk. He managed to convince him to revive the Yeomanry Light Car Patrols of the First World War, explaining that they needed to find out what the Italians might be up to beyond the Egyptian Sand Sea. Also they might engage in 'piracy', which appealed to Wavell, who had been lukewarm to the idea up to that point. He gave Bagnold six weeks to get his patrols off the ground, and he had carte blanche to obtain equipment with an order that all branches and heads of departments were to cooperate 'instantly and without question'.[4]

During the First World War the roles had been somewhat reversed: Italy and Britain were allies, while the Senussi Arabs were allied to the Turks. At the end of 1915 the border between Egypt and Libya was the scene of some skirmishes, when the Senussi – aided by Turkey and Germany – invaded Egypt reaching Mersa Matruh. The British responded with cavalry patrols, but the units, including Australian cavalry, found operations in this terrain away from the coastal strip to be difficult. Even switching to camels did not really solve the problem. For the Senussi camels were a way of life and they knew more about the terrain, which was virtually unmapped away from the coast.

To combat the Senussi the Yeomanry Light Car Patrols were set up in 1916. Using Model T Fords with oversized 3.5-inch tyres, these patrols were able to range well down into the desert, and learned how to operate there. Inventing new techniques of navigation and movement, surveying and mapmaking, they were finally able to clear the enemy from the frontiers and oases. By 1917 the war had moved on and the patrols were disbanded.[5]

During the Second World War most of the desert fighting took place within a narrow coastal strip. However to the south, beyond the oases of Siwa, Jarabub and Jalo lay the inner Libyan Desert, a huge expanse of territory larger than France and Spain put together, of which the Western Desert was mere edging. The desert was (and still is) uninhabited and without much life due to lack of rainfall. This was where the LRDG was to operate.

Within the inner desert the Italians had established a chain of military posts and landing grounds in their territory. They had also formed special colonial forces for duty there; the motorised 'Auto-Saharan' companies had the advantage of permanently attached reconnaissance aircraft. But the ground patrols were designed only to operate over reasonably good surfaces.

One chain of Italian posts, connected by a good track, went south to Jalo and Kufra and onto Uweinat, 600 miles inland, the nearest Italian post to the East African Empire 1000 miles away across the Sudan. When war came the garrisons of these posts continued their watch, feeling safe behind the natural barrier of the great Egyptian Sand Sea which lay to the east.

Bagnold knew that the Egyptian Sand Sea was not a complete obstacle to all forms of motor transport. However, the vast inland flank was unlikely ground to be used by the main armies; the great dunes could only be crossed at a few narrow places and the surfaces could not stand the passage of many vehicles. The patrols would have to be small and because of the distances involved, self sufficient. They needed great skill and confidence in 'finding their position astronomically, for the chance of being lost in almost lunar surroundings is a great deterrent to moving far away from reliable tracks.'[6]

Personnel was the first requirement. Bagnold sent for Pat Clayton and Bill Kennedy Shaw, neither of whom were serving in the army; the former was a surveyor in Tanganyika, the latter curator of the Palestine Museum in Jerusalem. These three men had all served in the First World War and were long in the tooth for the arduous tasks that lay ahead. Their companion Rupert Harding-Newman was somewhat younger; his job was to obtain vehicles and equipment.

As soon as Clayton and Kennedy Shaw arrived they were commissioned as captains. Bagnold recruited men from the newly arrived New Zealand Division, who, he felt, would be more at home with vehicles and machinery than home-grown troops.

For transport Harding-Newman obtained Chevrolet 30cwt trucks, modified to take loads of two tons with up-rated springs; the doors, windshields and body tops were stripped off. Carrying racks were fitted for extra fuel, water and radio sets and machine-gun mountings were welded on. A radiator condenser system was fitted to each vehicle in the form of a steel tank bolted to the step and connected to the radiator, both being sealed. When a radiator boiled – which happened frequently in the desert – the steam was condensed into the water in the condenser and as the radiator cooled the vacuum sucked it back inside. All modifications were carried out by American and Greek technicians at Chevrolet in Alexandria and at Fords in Cairo. Ten trucks were needed for a 40-man patrol unit, with each patrol carrying ten Lewis guns, four Boyes anti-tank rifles and one 37mm Bofors anti-aircraft gun, plus the usual infantry weapons of Bren guns, Sten guns and rifles.

The men were schooled in the problems of desert navigation by Kennedy-Shaw, who introduced them to the sun compass, one with which direction could be maintained despite the magnetic effect of vehicle bodies that could throw an ordinary compass as much as ten degrees out. Bagnold took the signals training, teaching the young New Zealanders the use of the army No 11 wireless sets, which according to the manual had a range of some 75 miles, but which he knew, from experience, could transmit Morse over 1000 miles across the desert at certain times of day. The New Zealanders were quick to learn, taking to their strange new life 'like ducks to water', recalled Bagnold.[7] After six weeks of tough training Wavell inspected the small unit and declared it fit for operations.

Clayton had already taken a small party on one valuable reconnaissance in August; he had discovered a second sand sea (the 'Libyan'[8]) to the east of the Jalo-Kufra, and had found a way across it. He watched the route for three days, discovering that the track had broken up and the Italians were using a track some 20 miles to the west. He also discovered a level plain to the north of Kufra within the horseshoe of the sand seas. During this time the main body set up dumps along the safe routes within Egyptian territory to the southwest of Cairo and across the Sand Sea as far out as the Gilf Kebir. These dumps contained everything that might be needed, and by laying them out the crews gained much first-hand experience in driving and navigation.

With the dumps ready and with Clayton's report on Italian activities, Bagnold felt it was time for his men to cross the Sand Sea. Kennedy-Shaw considered the prospect with mixed feelings.

> Late in the evening when the sands cool quickly and the dunes throw long shadows the Sand Sea is one of the most lovely things in the

world; no words can properly describe the beauty of those sweeping curves of sand. At a summer midday when the sun beats down all its shapes to one flat glare of sand and the sand-drift blows off the dune crests like the snow-plume off Everest, it is as good an imitation of Hell as one could devise. It was across 150 miles of this dead world that Bagnold was proposing to take for the first time a force of heavily loaded trucks.[9]

Just before the Italians launched their attack on Egypt, Bagnold and his evolving force set up their first base at Siwa Oasis on the Escarpment of the Qattara Depression. From here two patrols set out into enemy territory. One attacked Italian fuel dumps and landing grounds along the hard track south to Kufra, while the other – commanded by Clayton – went right through Italian-controlled territory into Chad, to make contact with the French forces at Fort Lamy. The appearance of the LRDG patrol convinced the garrison to join forces with the Free French and British.

This was all carried out in the heat of summer. Kennedy-Shaw observed, 'You don't merely feel hot, you don't merely feel tired, you feel as if every bit of energy had left you, as if your brain was thrusting its way through the top of your head and you want to lie in a stupor till the accursed sun has gone down.'[10] At midday they could do nothing but lie under their trucks in an attempt to find some relief from the blistering sun. However the first mission was a success, the patrols have covered around 4000 miles. Arriving back in Cairo, Wavell was delighted by his 'mosquito army' and promoted Bagnold to lieutenant-colonel and gave the go-ahead to expand the force.

In November 1940, Bagnold went to Fort Lamy to finish the negotiations Clayton had started with the garrison. Soon French troops were working alongside the LRDG, carrying out raids led by Clayton – now a major – against positions in the Murzuk Oasis region deep within Italian-held Libya. From Murzuk they tracked back east. Scouting ahead for a possible attack on Kufra, Clayton's patrol was spotted by enemy aircraft who strafed the vehicles. Not far away was a patrol of the Italian Auto-Saharan. Clayton was sitting in the last vehicle and was shot up. 'They got me on the head though the helmet prevented a wound, and punctured both front tyres and the radiator.'[11] Clayton was then wounded in the arm and his truck was disabled with hits to the fuel tank and engine. The Auto-Saharans closed in and he had no choice but to surrender. Clayton was taken to Kufra, then to a camp in Tripoli and finally to a POW camp in Italy.

Bagnold wrote to Clayton's wife Ellie, saying that the Italians would treat 'Pat' well, and that the success of the raid on Murzuk was entirely due to him. Lieutenant Bruce Ballantyne – who had been on the same patrol but evaded capture and returned safely to Cairo – described Clayton as 'always leading and showed no personal fear at all. He had one fault, and that was an over readiness to expose himself rather than risk casualties to his men.'[12]

7. Tripoli, March 1941

By the time Pat Clayton had reached his POW camp in Italy, Almásy and Ritter had arrived in Tripoli. Rommel had already been there for an initial reconnaissance, taking to the air on the afternoon of 12 February to examine what he called 'the soil of Africa'. He concluded, 'The flight confirmed me in my plan to fortify Sirte and the country on either side of the coast road and to reserve the motorised forces for mobile defence.'[1]

The new commander of German troops in Africa had been informed of his appointment by the Führer personally on the afternoon of 6 February. Adolf Hitler had already announced Führer order No22, after disaster had overtaken the Italian 10th Army: 'The position in the Mediterranean on strategically political and psychological grounds demands German aid. Tripolitania must be saved.' However, he saw it as a defensive move, insisting, 'It is not possible either for the Italians or for ourselves to launch an offensive against Egypt.'[2] At first only the 5th Light Division was sent to stiffen the Italians. Consisting of a panzer regiment and reconnaissance battalion, as soon as the magnitude of the disaster became apparent it was reinforced by the 15th Panzer Division.

On 19 March Rommel flew to Hitler's HQ to make his report; the Führer was friendly and awarded him the Oak Leaves to his Knight's Cross in recognition of outstanding leadership of the 7th Panzer Division in France the year before. They briefly discussed the situation in Africa, then Rommel was seen by the General Staff. He was told clearly that the High Command had no plans for decisive action against the British in North Africa, but he might conduct limited operations. Rommel however had his own ideas and already had a better understanding of German possibilities in the desert than those at OKW.

So as not to rub salt in Italian wounds, in theory Rommel was junior to the new Italian commander in Africa, General Italo Garibaldi. However, the staff of the Afrika Korps were soon drawing up plans for Operation *Sonnenblume* (*Sunflower*) – the deployment of German troops to North Africa – with little consideration of their allies, other than how best to exploit them. These plans were intended to throw the British back to Egypt, and ultimately to take the great prize of the Suez Canal and Cairo.

By this time the British Western Desert Force was dangerously depleted; its veteran troops, the Australian 6th Division and the newly arrived New Zealanders had all been sent to Greece. This left the British thin on the ground and no match for Rommel's panzers. Panzer Armee Afrika soon broke through what was no more than a border patrol by the 2nd Armoured Division and took Benghazi within three days. British Generals Philip Neame VC and Richard O'Connor were captured near Derna, and by 11 April – after less than a month – the Germans were besieging Tobruk.

Almásy and Ritter arrived in Tripoli in time to watch the panzers leaving, clanking east in a cloud of dust. With them they had a small crew of drivers and wireless operators, all handpicked Abwehr men operating within the framework of the Brandenburg Lehr Regiment. Admiral Canaris had told Ritter that his unit should 'work with but not for Rommel'.

***

Major Nikolaus Ritter had got wind of German intervention in Africa early in 1941. He rushed off to see Canaris, to try and sell him his plan to get General Aziz el Masri out of Egypt and set him up as a rallying voice for Arab nationalists. Canaris and Ritter had first met in 1937, soon after the latter had returned from the US. He had served in the First World War as an infantry officer, after which he went to the US in the 1920s to start a new life. He prospered in the textile business and married an American woman with whom he had two children. During the Depression his business suffered badly so he opted to return to the 'New Germany' where the future looked better. He needed an assisted passage to Germany and his application led to a summons and interview at the German Embassy in Washington, where, to his surprise, he was taken to the office of Lieutenant General Freidrich Von Boetticher, the military attaché. Boetticher suggested he should re-join the German Army, even though Ritter was 40. Back in Germany he was assigned to the Luftwaffe, and to the Abwehr's air intelligence unit in Hamburg. A strange posting, he remarked, 'as I knew nothing of flying or intelligence work.'

Ritter was even more astounded when, in July 1937, Admiral Canaris himself ordered him by signal to extend 'intelligence work immediately to cover the air force and aviation industry in the United States.' He was stunned by this.

> For the moment I forgot my surroundings and my new work. My life in the United States, with all its ups and downs, passed in review before my eyes. It was difficult to reconcile myself to the idea of working against the country which I loved best next to my own native land.[3]

Having got used to the idea, Ritter realised that the best person to go to the US was himself. He went to see Canaris personally to sell him the idea. In his writings Ritter gives the impression that he did not overly take to the head of the Abwehr. He found him 'colourless' and; 'his gestures were considered. He spoke carefully and softly. His eyes were an indefinable blue ... In short he was hard to describe.' Perhaps Canaris's inscrutable air irritated Ritter.[4]

The Admiral was opposed to Ritter going to America. The mission had followed a request from the Luftwaffe to try and obtain the design of the Norden bombsight, and eventually Ritter managed to convince Canaris that he was the best man for the job. He pointed out that he 'knew the country' spoke American English like a native and more importantly he 'had not been working at intelligence long enough for the Americans to be aware of it.' Canaris advised him to 'stay clear of all official Germans' for they had little 'understanding of our work'.

On 11 October 1937 Ritter boarded the *Bremen* at Bremerhaven for the trip to New York, where he arrived six days later. Ritter met his contact Hermann Lang, who worked as an inspector in a Manhattan factory making the Norden bombsights. Lang may have been disenchanted with the US as he had been waiting to become an American citizen for ten years. Being of German origin he was easy to recruit, and the Abwehr gave him the codename 'Paul'. His task was to take blueprints home (blueprints which should have been locked in a safe after use) and copy them, before returning them to the factory. His drawings were then smuggled out of the US in an umbrella. In the end it made only a small difference to the German war effort, as the Germans had developed a very similar sight, the Eagle Apparatus.

***

'My dear fellow, you can't be altogether right in the head' was the reaction of Canaris to Ritter's General El Masri scheme. 'It won't work. Forget it Ritter.' Yet four weeks later Canaris called Ritter at his Hamburg desk, saying he had reconsidered the scheme, and that Ritter had three weeks to get it off the ground. The next day Ritter was on his way to Budapest to see Almásy (see Chapter 2). Early in February the Major was back in Berlin at the Abwehr headquarters on Tirpitz Ufer reporting to Canaris, outlining the details of his plan. The Admiral approved them and Almásy and Ritter were on their way to North Africa.

The 'Ritter Commando' as it came to be known kicked its heels in Tripoli, and was soon 1000 miles behind the fluid front line. Almásy spent his time producing a military-geographical study of the Libyan Desert, and gave his expert advice to Rommel's staff on the use and modifications of vehicles and equipment for desert conditions.

The front line stabilised near the Egyptian frontier, the Afrika Korps tanks having run out of fuel. For days they had only managed to keep going with captured supplies of fuel and water. The 5th Light Division pushed on to Tobruk; on 7 April Churchill had telegraphed General Wavell: 'You should surely be able to hold Tobruk.'[5]

Ritter's small group moved forward to Derna on the Libyan coast to establish itself there. Almásy met Rommel for the first time and offered to lead a German battalion to Upper Egypt to start an insurrection amongst the Egyptian Army and population but Rommel apparently turned it down due to lack of vehicles and fuel.[6]

By this time Ritter and Almásy had come to the attention of the people at Bletchley Park, the Government Code and Cypher School in Buckinghamshire. The Abwehr's messages were being monitored by the Radio Security Service (RSS); Mavis Lever and Margaret Rock would later manage to reconstruct the main Abwehr cipher machine, and could read an Abwehr message by December 1941.[7] However even before this, Captain Hugh Trevor Roper, head of the RSS, managed to identify Ritter as 'a man of great importance'.[8]

Having settled at Derna, a small town on the coast where thousands of swallows had assembled for their annual spring migration to northern Europe, the commando began to set up Operation *El Masri*.

Radio contact was made with the Egyptian General, via a portable transmitter smuggled into the Hungarian Legation in Cairo inside a diplomatic bag. There an operator codenamed 'Martin' sent encoded reports to the Germans via Budapest, until the British persuaded the Egyptian government to withdraw diplomatic privileges from the 'nest of spies', which cut off communications.[9]

The transmitter was removed to the Hungarian Church of St Theresa in Shubra where it was hidden under the altar. The church and the mysterious Father Demetrios came to the attention of British Intelligence and it was observed that it was 'visited by many doubtful people'. The transmitter was used by the Father in Operation *El Masri*.[10]

Part III

OPERATIONS

8. The Troublesome General

GENERAL AZIZ EL MASRI HAD been Chief of Staff of the Egyptian Army and once a tutor to King Farouk. He was an ardent nationalist and open critic of the British, as well as a close friend of the Egyptian Prime Minister, Ali Maker. Many of his army officers were suspected of having contacts with the enemy.

With the entry of Italy into the war, the British Ambassador in Cairo, Sir Miles Lampson, demanded the removal of El Masri from command. However, Ali Maker did no more than put him on indefinite leave, and then only after the capture of the Italian headquarters in Libya in which was found a complete set of the British plans for the defence of Egypt. These plans were tracked back directly to a set supplied to El Masri. 'Sammy' Sansom was surprised at this to say the least: 'Why our plans should have been shown to General el Masri was, and still is, a mystery to me. He had never made any secret of his strong pro-Axis sympathies.' Even worse, the General's dismissal did not restrict him and he 'joined the ranks, already numerous, of Egyptians of high standing who were always likely to cause us trouble and whom we could not touch until they did.'[1] It was in Germany's interest to get hold of El Masri and use his influence in the Egyptian Army to bolster support for the Axis cause and focus anti-British sentiments.

Events in other parts of the Arab world were also coming into play. At the outbreak of the Second World War the young King of Iraq was only four years old, and his uncle, the pro-British Amir Abdul Illah, was regent. Iraq broke off diplomatic relations with Germany, but in June 1940 they did not break off relations with Italy. Thus the Italian legation at Baghdad became a centre of Arab nationalists and anti-British agitation. In August 1940 the German ambassador in Ankara, Franz Von Papen, met with Osman Kemal Haddad, the private secretary of the Grand Mufti. The Iraqi Ambassador was also present, the brother of the pro-Axis prime minister, Rashid Ali el-Ghailani.

Haddad, who was far from reliable, told Von Papen about the situation in Iraq and the wish for German aid under the same terms as Italy in order to throw off the British yoke, and an assurance that

they would support the independence of all mandated Arab countries. They also talked of a revolt in Palestine orchestrated from Syria,
to help the fight against the British. Moving on to Berlin, Haddad
presented himself at the Reich Foreign Office as some sort of ambassador for the Arab world. He advised them that a committee led by
the Grand Mufti was coordinating action.

At about the same time Eppler was in Istanbul, staying at the Pera
Palace Hotel, enjoying the favours of an 'oriental beauty – a doe-eyed
little darling' he was tiring of and trying to ditch. An Abwehr contact
told him to report to the embassy in Ankara, an ideal excuse to slip
away, which doubtless he told his mistress was a business trip. He was
off to find Hadji Mohammed Amin el Husseini, the Grand Mufti.

It was his first visit to the embassy, known locally as the 'German
Village'. There Eppler met 'Aladin' who had asked to see him; Eppler
thought he was 'one of the cleverest Abwehr agents, and his cover
name Aladin fitted him perfectly.' To avoid being overheard they went
for a drive, and stopping the car in a remote spot Aladin told Eppler
of Haddad's visit and that he was on his way to Berlin. Eppler told
him that the Grand Mufti 'had a finger in far too many pies in far too
many places' and that Haddad was not to be trusted.[2]

Aladin told Eppler of his new mission to go to Iraq and find out
what was going on, and whether a *putsch* was possible. Eppler had a
transmitter and the code would be taken from Wensinck's *The Muslim
Creed*. They would start with page 4, skip a page a day, and use the
second paragraph.

Eppler travelled slowly south by train across the Middle East
using his Egyptian passport. He soon realised that the anti-British
mood was beginning to cool. However, the word from Iraq was that
the army remained pro-Axis and a group of officers known as the
'Golden Square' were conspiring to start a rebellion.

Arriving in Baghdad he found the city 'dusty' and smelly and it had
lost 'the glories of bygone days'. There he met with prominent Iraqis
in the villa of Sheikh Djafar in the northern part of the city on the
left bank of the Tigris, shaded by tall date palms.

> A servant, stepping like a stork, carried his tray over the legs of the
> guests scattered around the room. It was all very Arab. The assembled
> company gave the impression of having just been awakened from a

long nightmare of slavery. But I knew them, these cunning bastards,
and I knew that they were well off.

He knew they expected him to be able, through the Germans, to
supply the power to 'blow' the British out of Iraq. 'Then the great
independence jamboree could begin.'

Eppler observed that one man deliberately arrived five minutes
late, seemingly for dramatic effect. It was the Grand Mufti, 'the world
champion of intrigue'. He took the place of honour, a throne-like
chair, 'vulgar and tasteless, with plenty of gold and tinsel' with green
upholstery. He greeted them all as if he was giving a private audience.

Eppler disliked him, and he did not consider himself a conspirator,
more an observer, as he counted nine in the room excluding himself.
Those gathered seemed sure that the British knew nothing of their
aims. Eppler was not convinced on that score, and was even more
alarmed that they felt they could overcome any obstacle with the
help of Allah; after all they had the Grand Mufti to guide them.

There was much debate but the Mufti was pulling all the strings.
He said that the Italians were with them and he expected the
Germans to do likewise. His agent was in Berlin. He was in constant
contact with revolutionary groups in Palestine, Syria and Egypt. But
alas, the insurgents were very poor and needed support. Apparently
at this point the Mufti looked directly at Eppler, smiling, but Eppler
made no comment; 'For me the afternoon was not worth even a two
line report.' When the meeting broke up Eppler met with Colonel
Mahmoud Salman, an air force officer and member of the 'Golden
Square'. He felt rather like Eppler and was equally unenthusiastic
about Husseini the Grand Mufti.

Eppler sent a downbeat report to his superiors the next day. He
had seen much evidence of British troop movements (this was
February 1941), moving through Iraq for 'the North African Front'
and he decided to leave for Egypt via Damascus, as he had completed
his mission.[3]

In early April 1941 the Regent of Iraq learnt of a plot to arrest him
and fled Baghdad to Habbaniya from where he flew to Basra, taking
refuge on HMS *Cockchafer*. The Iraqi Prime Minister, Rashid Ali el
Ghalani – with the support of the 'Golden Square' made up of army
and air force officers – seized power. The new British Ambassador Sir

Kinahan Cornwallis only reached Baghdad the day before the coup. It had been hoped he might have been able to douse the flames of revolution by diplomatic means.[4]

The rebels besieged the air training base at Habbaniya, and surrounded the British Embassy in which 300 people were trapped. The Middle East Commander in Chief General Archibald Wavell already had the German invasion of Greece and Rommel's dash across Cyrenaica to deal with, and had no troops to spare for Iraq.[5] However, the Chiefs of Staff were in favour of armed intervention and General Sir Claude Auchinleck, Commander in Chief India, offered to send a brigade to Iraq, which within a month could be up to a division in strength, and which he was willing to command. But Churchill would not transfer the responsibility for Iraq from Wavell; the Prime Minister constantly bullied and harried his reserved Middle East commander whom he found baffling. Churchill considered Wavell no more than 'a good chairman of a Tory Association'.[6]

Wavell favoured a diplomatic solution but he scraped together various units to make 'Habforce', which entered Iraq through Palestine in mid May. It consisted of one mechanised brigade of the 1st Cavalry Division, one field regiment and a lorry-borne infantry division. It had no armoured cars, tanks, anti-aircraft guns or anti-tank weapons, and in Wavell's opinion it would be too weak and too late.[7]

Meanwhile the Abwehr Operation *El Masri* was coming together. It was decided that Almásy would pilot a Heinkel III German medium bomber specially adapted for a long range role, with RAF markings. He would fly low and slip under British radar and pick up the General at Red Jebel, an elevated plateau southwest of Cairo.

This was not the first scheme put forward to get El Masri out of Egypt, all of which largely descended into a comedy of errors. The first idea had been to send a U-boat into Lake Burullus, east of Alexandria, where one of the branches of the Nile flows into the Mediterranean. That was until someone pointed out the lake was far too shallow for any submarine. Next was a suggested rendezvous near Kataba on the fringe of the desert, until it was realised the British had a large supply dump there and many troops in the area.

On the night of 16/17 May Almásy took off from Derna in Libya, heading for Red Jebel, accompanied by another Heinkel III. The pick-up point was not far from the road to Cairo, and was supposed to have been marked by a giant white cross. According to Ritter, Almásy and his wing man were forced to fly far out into the desert to avoid British standing air patrols.

> Everything went according to schedule. They saw the Red Jebel and they expected to find the landing cross of the Pasha.
>
> But there was no landing cross. Their disappointment was great, their excitement grew. What could they do?[8]

They waited as long as possible, crossing and re-crossing the area in case El Masri was nearby or lost. But with fuel running low they were forced to return to base. Almásy did not seem in the least upset according to Ritter, the former feeling sure that the 'Pasha' would not have deliberately let them down. They would have to wait for the next morning's broadcast from their contacts to learn what had happened.

In the event it was not 'Martin' – their radio contact in Cairo who had helped organise the flight of El Masri from Egypt – who called; rather they learnt from Radio Cairo that the General had been arrested. Later it was indicated that El Masri had taken off from Cairo that night with the cover story that he was bound for Baghdad to persuade pro-German Iraqi officers of the 'Golden Square' to abandon their anti-British revolution. Some accounts say the aircraft broke down and had to make a forced landing.[9]

Sansom tells a different story; some time after 2 May he was told by informants within the Egyptian Army that El Masri was defecting to the Germans. He raced off to the airfield by car, arriving just as the plane was taxiing to take off, accompanied by Colonel Hegazi, Chief of Egyptian Army Intelligence, as in theory Sansom had no power over Egyptian nationals. They chased the aircraft down the runway, Sansom exhorting his driver to go faster, even though they knew it was hopeless. 'The aircraft was heading into the wind and almost at the point of take-off.' They managed to get up alongside the plane for a brief few seconds before it left them behind. 'We saw the tail of the aircraft lift. In seconds now the wheels would leave the ground and the machine would be airborne, but still we hurtled on.' Yet the plane did not take off; perhaps the pilot panicked or tried to lift off too early. The tail dropped, the aircraft slewed around and hit the boundary fence, the starboard wing hitting a concrete post. The tail rose into the air burying the propeller into the earth and the aircraft, a twin-engine bomber, came to rest on its smashed starboard side.

They helped the occupants from the wreckage and Hegazi arrested El Masri and his companions. Back at his headquarters they interviewed the General, who refused to answer any questions in the presence of Sansom, the representative of a 'foreign power'. 'As this was not getting us anywhere I left,' said Sansom.

> I had nothing to complain about, anyway. Helped very largely by luck … we had spoiled the General's escape attempt and this prevented the establishment of a 'Free Egyptian Army' on German-occupied territory. Hegazi told me afterwards that the contents of the general's briefcase made it clear that was the design.

Colonel Hegazi informed Sansom of the other escape plans – including the U-boat at Lake Burullus – that El Masri had told him about, but it is likely he was far from telling the whole truth even then.[10] The wily General had even suggested to a British Special Operations Executive Officer, Colonel Cudbert Thornhill, when they had lunched together on 12 May, that he be given official sanction to fly to Baghdad on a mission to stop the officers' revolt there. Thornhill denied that he ever agreed to any plan but even lunching with El Masri was enough to get him sent back to London in disgrace, at the insistence of an angry Ambassador Lampson.[11]

After the war El Masri met Ritter in Cairo and spun him all sorts of yarns, even describing an escape to Syria. But all the dates were wrong for he had been languishing in prison. It is fairly certain that the plane crash Sansom witnessed was on the night of 16/17 May and El Masri was trying to rendezvous with Almásy. A Middle East Intelligence report of 22 May endorses Sansom's account that El Masri tried to escape

> … on the night of 16/17 May, possibly to Syria en route to Iraq, in an Egyptian Air Force plane. With two officers, Hussein Zulficer Sabri and Abdul Moreim Abd ur Ru'uf [Sansom calls him Abdel Ra'ouf]. But the aircraft made a forced landing only ten miles from Cairo.[12]

However it appears that at some point El Masri escaped or was released by Colonel Hegazi, for on 19 May the Egyptian government issued a notice revealing that Aziz el Masri and two air force officers had committed an offence against the nation's safety and security. A reward of £1000 was to be paid to anyone who assisted in securing the arrest of one or all of the fugitives and that anyone harbouring them or helping them to escape would be severely punished. After a tip-off they were arrested in a suburb of Cairo on 6 June.[13]

There was much vocal support for El Masri amongst the local population; the General became an embarrassment to the Egyptian and British governments, but Lampson was reluctant to have the case dropped, a view shared by Anthony Eden, the British Foreign Secretary. Legal machinations delayed his trial in order to keep him locked up and court proceedings were continually put off and finally quietly dropped.

Sansom found out that El Masri's companion Abdel Ra'ouf was a member of the Muslim Brotherhood, who joined the growing file on 'Subversive Elements' within the Egyptian Army.

> Sometimes, in the evenings, I sat in my office with the dossiers spread in front of me, pored over the information and stared at the photographs as if by sheer concentration I could discover which of them were the leaders of the group.
>
> My favourite suspect was a short, slight young signals officer with a sleepy look that came from heavy lidded eyes. His name was Anwar el Sadat.[14]

Eppler was in Egypt in the early months of 1941, following his trip to Iraq. Checking on his contacts in Alexandria and Cairo, he observed: 'Our jobs were changing. Up until now the business of collecting information had been something of a game.' The people he knew 'were far from anticipating an Axis victory'.[15]

By early May he had moved on and was staying in the opulence of the Orient Palace Hotel in Damascus, opposite the Hejaz railway station. The station had been built in 1917, in readiness hopefully to ferry Muslim pilgrims to Medina in Saudi Arabia and then onward to Mecca. At breakfast he read in a newspaper that a rebellion had broken out in Iraq, which might mean a holy war against the British spreading across the Middle East. According to the editorial the British Consulate in Damascus had been attacked. Eppler rushed off to see for himself but discovered that the report was inaccurate.

He decided to take the Nairn bus to Baghdad, a journey of nearly 850 kilometres east across the flat and featureless Syrian desert. The Nairn service had been started by two New Zealanders, Gerry and Norman Nairn, who had served in the transport division of the same British Army that had thrown the Turks and their German allies out of Baghdad in 1917. Before the Nairn service the British had got to Baghdad by mail ship through the Suez Canal to land at Basra.

The Nairns proved the overland route in 1923, taking two Dodge cars from Beirut via Damascus to Baghdad. They won the postal contract, and a passenger service soon followed. Most of the journey was on hard natural surfaces where the vehicles could reach 50mph but even carrying iced drinks and vast quantities of food it was uncomfortable and tedious. Agatha Christie took the bus in 1928 and found the ride had a similar motion to a ship; she soon came down with travel sickness.

> The 48-hour trip across the desert was fascinating and rather sinister. It gave one the curious feeling of being enclosed rather than surrounded by a void. One of the things I was to realise was that at noon it was impossible to tell whether you were going north, south, east, or west, and I learnt that it was at this time of the day when the big six-wheeled cars most often ran off the track.[16]

The Nairns were long gone by 1941 but the bus bearing their name still ran. 'The interior stank as usual of garlic, onions and caraway seeds.' Eppler found little evidence of the 'Holy War', other than columns of British troops on the move.

In Ramadi, 100 miles west of Baghdad, a British officer stopped the bus and ordered the driver to take a different route into the city. Eppler found Baghdad in great confusion when he arrived on 4 May, the Iraqi soldiers almost helpless against RAF air attacks. The Mufti was behind the scenes immersed in 'political wheeling and dealing'. He found it 'a complete mess, no telling what's going on'.[17]

The Iraqi rebels attempted to besiege the RAF air training base at Habbaniya some 60 miles west of Baghdad. The units there were commanded by Air Vice Marshal H.G. Smart, a motley collection of obsolete and training aircraft, 78 in all. Many of these had been converted to a bomber role in expectation of hostilities, as the situation in Greece and Libya meant there were limited resources for reinforcement. However six Gladiators did arrive and 300 men of the King's Own Royal Regiment were flown in.

The Iraqis were soon in possession of the plateau overlooking the Habbaniya base, but dug in rather than moving forward. Smart knew the British were on their own, and the cantonment was hard to defend and was crammed with refugees. The British Ambassador – who was besieged in the Embassy in Baghdad[18] – informed Smart that he regarded the Iraqi threat to the base as an act of war.

At dawn on 2 May all available aircraft at Habbaniya attacked the Iraqi positions on the plateau, along with eight Wellingtons flying from Shaibah near Basra. Smart then expanded his attack to knock out the Iraqi Air Force. On the first day the Flying School made 193 sorties, and three days later the King's Own raided the plateau. By 6 May the Iraqis started pulling back from their positions. By mid-May Habforce was moving west from Palestine, while General Sir Claude Auchinleck's Indian troops came in from the southeast, quelling the rebellion.

A handful of Axis aircraft did arrive in Iraq, flying via Rhodes and Syria, fourteen ME 110 fighters, seven HE III bombers and twelve CR 42 Italian fighters. By 29 May the small force had lost 23 of their aircraft, and there were no more to spare with the Luftwaffe fully committed to the battle for Crete. On the next day came the news of the collapse of Rashid Ali's interim rebel government; he complained bitterly about the lack of support from the Axis and blamed them for everything.[19]

For the British it was the one bright spot amidst a sea of troubles. The garrison at Habbaniya had shown great fortitude and ingenuity under Smart's resolute leadership.

> In Baghdad the British civilians owed much to the firmness and tact of the Ambassador in his extremely difficult position, and some of them had good reason to be grateful to the United States Minister who gave them refuge at the worst time.[20]

By the third week in May Eppler had seen enough and headed for the mountains of Kurdistan and the Persian frontier. It was an area he had got to know well on a 1937 mission to canvas the tribes there on anti-British feeling.

As for the two heroes of the *putsch*, they had long ago crossed the Persian frontier and made their way to the safety of the Japanese Legation in Teheran. Rashid Ali el-Ghailam was eventually smuggled out of Persia via Turkey and on to Berlin. But the Mufti had greater difficulty in escaping and barely managed to get himself to Italy and then Berlin by November 1941.[21]

9. Exit Ritter

RITTER AND ALMÁSY DID NOT dwell on the El Masri fiasco. On 27 May Ritter's little force reported to Abwehr HQ in Hamburg that 'Imminent success in sight.' This was picked up by the British Radio Security Service.[1] The Ritter Commando was largely in the dark. Yet there was an efficient Italian network of spies in Cairo led by an officer called 'Nani'. The Abwehr had introduced 'Roberto' from their Athens branch into this cell and from May 1941 to January 1942 profited from his information. But somehow they did not quite trust the Italians; they were not 'reliable'. Canaris was keen to help Rommel; 'His strategy is based on ruse and surprise. Any information that helps him is worth more than 20 tanks, which, by the way, he is not getting anyway because they are being sent to Russia.'[2]

Ritter flew to Berlin in early June to arrange the next mission and to collect two spies named Muhlenbruch (codename Pat) and Klein (codename Patachon), nicknamed after two Danish comedians, one fat, one thin. Both agents were fluent in Arabic, having lived in Arab countries for years, Muhlenbruch in Haifa and Klein in Alexandria. They were to return to these cities to install secret transmitters and build up spy cells.

The plan was for the agents to be flown to a remote spot, from where they could make their way to their appointed cities without raising suspicion. Almásy planned a caravan route that led from the Farafrah Oasis to Deirut on the Nile. Some 60 miles from the river was a prominent hill, a good landmark. To the south of this the ground was firm, a perfect place for the aircraft to land. However, that left the agents with 60 miles of desert to cover. Neither man was young, one being 40 and the other close to 50. Again, Almásy came up with the solution, in the shape of a motorcycle, a light machine of Italian origin.

On 17 June two Heinkel bombers were at Derna, ready to transport the agents to the desert. One carried Ritter, the two spies and a motorcycle, the other was to fly escort. Things did not start well; the aircraft that was to carry the agents had a burst tyre.[3] Ritter ordered the agents and motorcycle to be swapped to the covering aircraft, while the damaged plane would cover. Almásy objected to this, worried that the pilot Guenther Raydt was not experienced in desert flying, and suggested that the pilots be changed, but Ritter would hear of no further delays. Almásy felt the whole thing was too risky and refused to take part. He was left behind.[4]

They took off and maintained a low altitude but crossing the border into Egypt they had to climb to 12,000 feet to avoid a sandstorm. Meanwhile Klein and Muhlenbruch slept in the bomb bay. After five hours the landmark hill chosen by Almásy was spotted and the aircraft descended to a few hundred feet. The sun was already low in the west. The escort aircraft circled above at 3000 feet but Raydt hesitated to land the other plane, which was carrying the agents. Captain Leicht, the observer, urged him to put the machine down. Still the pilot hesitated; the light was fading fast. Eventually they laid a smoke bomb to gauge the wind direction and Raydt came into land but pulled up at the last minute. He had spotted a British scout car on the horizon, revealed by its trail of dust.[5]

This meant another sweep of the area and landing approach. More delay. Again they approached the landing area. But the fading light was casting long shadows and Raydt would not risk it, saying that the ground was too bumpy. Leicht ordered him to try again but by this time the sun had gone down and the ground was invisible. By now Ritter was on the flight deck; he and Leicht urged the young pilot to land but he would not, saying that he was responsible for the safety of the aircraft and the people on it.

Leicht suggested that the agents jump, but this was out of the question. Ritter decided to postpone the mission, hoping that the 10th Air Corps – who had provided the aircraft and crews – would do so again. Ritter was bitterly disappointed, and no doubt reflected on Almásy's objections.

The two aircraft turned back for Derna. By this time Muhlenbruch had come up to the flight deck, wondering what was happening, only to hear that the mission was off for the time being. Then there was more bad news. 'No permission to land at Derna. Enemy Attack. Fly to alternative field,' reported the radio operator.

They had been flying over eight hours; did they have enough fuel to reach Benghazi 200 miles away? Shortly after this the port engine of the main aircraft began to misfire and they lost the variable pitch. They had no choice but to land at Derna. Then they were amongst the British aircraft and friendly flak. Evasive action was necessary but there was no news from Derna. There was an emergency landing strip on the coast but they could not find it and their fuel was almost gone. It was decided that they would have to ditch in the sea; Leicht told the pilot, 'Don't forget to keep your tail down when you land in the water.'[6]

They sent out an SOS, then hit the water. 'All we could hear was the howl of the wind over the wings,' says Ritter. 'The motors had stopped altogether. Suddenly there was a blow as hard as steel.'[7] The Heinkel III floated at first, her empty fuel tanks giving some buoyancy. Inside the aircraft, Ritter had a broken right arm, Leicht had broken ribs and Klein a badly bruised arm and shoulder. The pilot, radio operator and flight engineer were uninjured. Muhlenbruch was dead. The radio operator tried to get him out of the sinking aircraft, but found that he had been crushed to death by a crate.

The injured men, although in great pain, managed to swim away from the cockpit, which was steadily filling with water. The others had made the rubber dinghy seaworthy and quickly got Leicht and Ritter on board. Meanwhile the plane sank nose first, taking Muhlenbruch with it.

The survivors spent twelve hours in the water. Four men sat in the dinghy, the uninjured men paddling the craft as best they could, while two of the fitter men hung onto the safety lines in the water. They tried to steer due south. About midday the next day they came ashore between Barce and Derna.

They set off across the desert, suffering terribly from thirst for another 24 hours until they stumbled across an Arab village. There they were picked up by a Feiseler Storch light aircraft of the Desert Rescue Squadron.[8]

Meanwhile the escort Heinkel had managed to land at Benina, very low on fuel. Almásy reported this to Abwehr HQ, a message which was read by the British.[9]

Ritter was soon in the field hospital at Derna where his right arm was put in a cast – much to his relief, as the doctors had considered amputating the badly mangled limb.

I felt that to a great extent I had myself to blame for the failure. Initially, for switching the planes, and then for not having ordered Almásy to take my place. He might have been able to persuade the timid pilot to land. We had lost a valuable plane ... not to speak of the loss of [Muhlenbruch] ... It seemed that my lucky star had deserted me.[10]

Ritter and Leicht were soon flown to Athens in a Red Cross plane. Before leaving, Ritter handed over the leadership of the commando to Almásy. He promised that he would do as much for him as he could once he got back to Berlin, and advised, 'Now you must proceed with our alternate plan to take the next pair of agents by car across the desert.'[11]

Once in Berlin, Ritter, although still recovering, did not waste time, instructing Almásy to report 'to TirpitzFührer 80' – a message which was intercepted by the British RSS – where the next operation would be reviewed.[12]

When Ritter had recovered he wanted to lead the desert operation himself, but Canaris seemed to have lost confidence in him and declined, preferring to give Almásy sole command of what was to be called Operation *Salam*.[13] Almásy's abilities were not going unnoticed by the Allies either. British Intelligence MI6 had already identified him as a likely leader of a German LRDG using 'captured British Bren carriers and Ford V8 lorries'.[14]

10. Under the Pagoda Tree

BY JUNE 1941 THE BRITISH were just hanging on to their position in the Mediterranean and Middle East. Egypt remaining the fulcrum of this position; Cairo had already gone through two crises when it braced itself for the imminent arrival of Axis forces and the British prepared to evacuate. Even at this low point the British intelligence services are often portrayed in histories of the period as being far ahead of the Axis services. In one aspect they were: code breaking.

On 22 May 1941 the British code breakers, recently relocated to Bletchley Park, broke the Luftwaffe version of the Enigma machine cipher, the Enigma being an electro-mechanical rotary machine that generated codes to encrypt messages. From this time on they were able to read German traffic almost without a break for the remainder of the war. Churchill called his cryptanalysts 'the geese who laid the golden eggs and never cackled.'[1]

From June 1941 the term 'Ultra Secret' was used by the British for intelligence resulting from this decryption; the codename 'Ultra' is said to have been the idea of Commander Geoffrey Colpays. It was taken from the fact that the code breaking success was considered more important than the highest security classification at the time (Most Secret) and so was regarded as being Ultra Secret.[2]

Yet these advantages had really only borne fruit at the naval battle of Matapan in March 1941. Indeed the Ultra decodes may have made the British over-confident in their defence of Crete. On 6 May the Bletchley Park code breakers identified the probable date of completion of German preparations as 17 May and had the complete final operation orders for the execution of the assault. Churchill could hardly contain himself, believing the information to be priceless.

The British Chiefs of Staff certainly did discuss the Ultra Enigma evidence. All would have known about the part Ultra had played in Admiral A.B.C. Cunningham's victory at Matapan, but things were not so clear cut with regards to Crete. There were also concerns about Iraq, Cyprus and Syria.[3]

Wavell had been well aware of the adverse effect on the Western Desert Force of the requirement to support Greece, but even he was appalled by what he found on his first visit to the area on 16 March 1941. He found the escarpment running south from Benghazi and parallel to the coast to be a poor defensive line; nothing resembling the cliff-like position his subordinate generals had led him to believe. It was merely a line of sloping hills, no real obstacle to the enemy. Also the troops were too widely scattered, unable to give mutual support if attacked. The armoured forces on which the defence relied were in a poor state. The 2nd Armoured Division consisted of only one brigade of cruiser tanks, the other having gone to Greece, and of its 52 tanks, half were in the workshops, having exceeded both their track and engine mileages. Indeed, the men of the 6th RTR were better off with their captured M13 Italian tanks, which were more reliable.[4]

Lieutenant-General Philip Neame VC had become commander of the Western Desert Force as it was whittled away. Wavell found Neame 'pessimistic and asking for all kinds of reinforcements which I hadn't got. And his tactical dispositions were just crazy …'[5] He ordered Neame to pull his forces back to the highest positions and to tighten his defences.

> I came back anxious and depressed from this visit, but there was nothing much I could do about it. The movement to Greece was in full swing and I had nothing left in the bag. But I had foreboding and my confidence in Neame was shaken.[6]

Returning to his HQ in Cairo, Wavell had time to reflect on what faced his opponent Erwin Rommel. He felt, especially in view of the ever-increasing volume of Ultra decodes arriving daily from Bletchley Park, that he knew pretty much what German units and formations had arrived in North Africa. He concluded it would take until May for the main German force – the 15th Panzer Division – to arrive, a force for which Rommel would surely have to wait before making his move. Wavell felt that time was on his side; he hoped to send substantial reinforcements to Neame by then. He knew of Rommel's reputation for swift action, but even he 'could not ignore the iron laws of logistics. But Wavell did not yet know Rommel.'[7]

Wavell was not alone in misjudging Rommel, for his own Commander-in-Chief, Von Brauchitsch, and Hitler, took much the same view. Rommel was one of the most energetic of commanders. He spent hundreds of hours in the air over the desert on personnel reconnaissance. On the ground he could often be found near the front of fluid battles, narrowly avoiding capture or death on several occasions.

Evidence of his character can be found in the huge number of letters he wrote to his wife. He had first met Lucie Maria Mollin in 1911; they were engaged in 1915 and married a year later. He was happiest with her and their son. When separated he endeavoured, even in the heat of battle, to write to her every day. These letters show just how much he took upon himself.

***

5 March 1941

Dearest Lu,

Just back from a two-day journey – or rather flight – to the front, which is now 450 miles away to the east. Everything going fine.

A lot to do. Can't leave here for the moment as I couldn't be answerable for my absence. Too much depends on my own person and driving power. I hope you have some post from me.[8]

Rommel was also deeply interested in all forms of intelligence. The Radio Monitoring Platoon *(Horchzug)* Africa arrived on 25 February, 3rd Company, 56th Signals Battalion. It was fully deployed by 24 April and operating near the front line at Tobruk and the Egyptian border. The Germans enjoyed superiority in radio interception for a good part of the North African Campaign.

The *Horchzug's* CO was Lieutenant Alfred Seebohm. His evaluation work would become legendary in the Afrika Korps, garnering the esteem of Rommel himself, as well as his operations staff. The value placed on the work of this company commander is shown by an order issued by the G-2 Intelligence Officer and Operations Staff in January 1942.

Radio monitoring will be carried out by German and Italian intercept troops.

The assignment of German intercept troops to be organised by Lieutenant Seebohm, CO 3/N56.

The assignment of Italian intercept troops is to be organised by the Information Officer (SIM) of Supercommando of the Italian Forces in North Africa.

The assignment of German intercept section and platoons as well as the evaluation of their results to be controlled by Lieutenant Seebohm only.

The use of the Italian and German Signals units to intercept enemy messages is to be confined to enemy combat reports.

All ciphers and wireless documents captured from the enemy are of the utmost importance and are to be handed over as quickly as possible to headquarters Panzergruppe Afrika

For the Commander of the Panzergruppe
The Chief of the General Staff
Signed Colonel Westphal[9]

Apart from radio monitoring, Rommel was also keen to recruit agents to bolster his intelligence resources. But in the uninhabited wastes of Libya these were not available. The reports of Arab nomads were of dubious value and the inhabitants of the coastal areas hated the Italians, a dislike that extended to their German allies. They were more inclined to help the British, although they had a general contempt for all the mad foreigners.

Therefore in March 1941 Rommel had to rely almost exclusively on his own reconnaissance flights for information on the enemy. What he saw was the British pulling back to the escarpment and digging in. This convinced him that the British were not about to interfere with the deployment of the Afrika Korps. He was well aware of the diversity of Wavell's command. The initiative was his, which he was quick to seize. On 3 April he wrote to his wife:

Dearest Lu

> We've been attacking since the 31st with dazzling success. There'll be
> consternation amongst our masters in Tripoli and Rome, perhaps in
> Berlin too. I took the risk against all orders and instructions because
> the opportunity seemed favourable …[10]

Wavell flew up to Barce on 2 April, having realised that Rommel was
not acting as predicted, but doubting Neame's messages of doom. He
did not think Rommel could have organised a force capable of occupying the whole of Cyrenaica; perhaps he was conducting a large raid.
He found chaos and the next day ordered General O'Connor up to
assist Neame.

On 6 April Germany invaded Greece and Yugoslavia. In the
Western Desert that night, after two days of fruitless efforts trying
to coordinate the army, Neame and O'Connor decided to pull their
headquarters back from Maraua. Even the experienced O'Connor
could do little to stem the tide. The 2nd Armoured Division was
falling apart.

They set off in Neame's white Cadillac staff car, the General at
the wheel as his driver was exhausted. They got lost well after midnight and headed north toward Derna instead of heading east. With
O'Connor and Colonel John Combe asleep in the back, they ran into
a German force that had just cut the Derna road. For them the war
was over. The capture of Sir Richard O'Connor, a talented officer,
was a disaster for the Western Desert Force.[11] Command devolved
to Brigadier John Harding who had been travelling a little in front
of Neame's car and had passed the point on the Derna road minutes
before the Germans arrived.

By now Rommel had been officially let off the leash. Hitler had
countermanded the German High Command's order for a 'limited
offensive', giving Rommel the fullest freedom of action. However,
Tobruk held. The town had been fortified by the Italians and the
Australian defenders had had a little time to catch their breath
and organise themselves. The Germans got involved in a difficult
infantry fight; Blitzkrieg tactics were no good and even Rommel's
energy was not enough. For nine days he tried to take the city until
sandstorms, heavy tank losses and the death of two of his most

effective commanders obliged him to think again. The defenders of Tobruk did much to restore British morale by their stoic display. A month later the soldier's magazine *Parade* was dedicated to 'The Spirit of Tobruk'.[12]

Rommel had to leave the best harbour in Cyrenaica to the British, a thorn in his side, compounding the strain on his overextended supply lines. But he was loath to give up the initiative. Leaving a besieging force behind, by mid-May Sollum had fallen and he had reached the Halfaya Pass, the gateway to Egypt.

All the while Wavell had to deal with the retreat from Greece, the defence of Crete and revolutions in Iraq and Syria. For once, Churchill sympathised with his commander. There was no nagging or recriminations; practical aid was the order of the day. He stripped the home defence, sending 300 tanks and 50 Hurricane fighters by fast convoy to Alexandria, which they reached on 12 May.[13]

On 27 April General Friedrich Paulus, who would later gain immortality at Stalingrad, arrived at Rommel's desert HQ. He had been dispatched by a concerned General Franz Halder, Chief of the General Staff (OKH), to find out just what Rommel was up to as he 'has not sent in a single clear report, and I have the feeling that things are in a mess …'[14]

On his arrival Paulus cancelled an attack on Tobruk scheduled for 30 April but later relented and let it go ahead. The attack failed and Paulus advised that no further attacks should be made. He reported to OKH on 12 May 'that the D.A.K. was in difficulties tactically, and that the supply situation was most unsatisfactory. Strong action was necessary, he thought, if a serious crisis was to be avoided.'[15]

Within hours Bletchley Park had decoded the Paulus report. Churchill's and to a lesser extent Wavell's reaction was positive. There could be an opportunity here; pressure could be applied to bring the 'crisis' to fruition and Tobruk could be relieved. Thus Operation *Brevity* was born. It began on 15 May and lasted some 36 hours, but failed. The trouble was that Rommel and his army did not quite see it the way Paulus did, and by the end of the fighting the British had achieved little. Moreover the Afrika Korps had begun to learn the value of using the 88mm anti-aircraft gun in an anti-tank role, as demonstrated by the burnt out British tanks littering the area around the Halfaya Pass.

The 88mm gun was even more effective during the British offensive Operation *Battleaxe*, which began on 15 June, utilising the reinforcements Churchill had hurried to what he called 'The Nile Army'. British command could not comprehend the fast-moving battle and within two days, in fighting around Sollum, had lost hundreds of tanks for no gain.

It was down to the Chief of Staff Lieutenant-General Sir Arthur Smith to deliver a telegram to Wavell on 22 June, telling him that he was to exchange appointments with Auchinleck. The General agreed with Churchill that the job needed 'a new head and a new hand'. He hoped for some leave, but the Prime Minister wanted him in New Delhi to take up his post as Commander-in-Chief India, where, as he put it, he could rest 'sitting under the pagoda tree'.[16]

11. The 'Good Source'

IN THE SUMMER OF 1941 'Sammy' Sansom and his team hardly had time to bemoan the loss of Wavell. Freya Stark was with a small group who saw Wavell off at the airport, the atmosphere amongst the small group of well wishers, she felt, was one of 'loyalty and devotion'.[1]

On 22 June Germany launched the invasion of Russia, Operation *Barbarossa*. 'Suddenly' wrote Sansom 'all the communists in the world were transferred to our side.' But there was no communism in Egypt at that time to muddy the waters.[2]

> That summer of 1941 was pretty trying, with Rommel poised on the frontier and a constant stream of our chaps coming in from the desert for a brief spell of leave ... but too many of them got drunk and shouted the odds about how they were going to deal with the Huns when they got back.

Sansom did not mind the ordinary Tommies having a good time, but the officers were more of a worry, as they openly talked about military matters in bars and clubs, despite the many signs bearing the famous line 'Careless Talk Costs Lives'.

> I had one of my NCOs stationed almost permanently in the bar at Shepheard's [Hotel], and his particular unsolved mystery of the war was whether or not the Swiss barman, Joe, was an enemy spy. If he was he was brilliant. I watched him several times myself, and never saw him budge when one of his officer customers dropped his voice to tell his drinking companion a confidence. I thought probably Joe was innocent; I do not suppose he looked any more guileless than Mac [the barman] at the Kit Kat cabaret.[3]

Meanwhile Eppler had spent a few happy months with Sonia in Copenhagen during the summer. He had completed a refresher course in Brandenburg east of Berlin, home of the Brandenburg Regiment. This unit was developed by Hauptmann Theodor Van

Hippel, and was part of the Abwehr 2nd Department. It initially consisted mainly of former German expatriates, like Eppler, fluent in foreign languages.

Returning to Ankara he met 'Aladin' in a Turkish bath, for cover, which Eppler found uncomfortable, 'trying to get the whole business over with oriental equanimity'. Aladin seemed to revel in the 'torture'.[4] He confided to Aladin that he had been in Spain, and he felt that he 'ran around Iraq for nothing and I wasted my time in Afghanistan and Persia too.' It had quenched his thirst for adventure but like most of his missions, 'it seemed a failure.'[5] However, he felt he might have stumbled across some useful information some time after the failed revolt in Iraq.

In January 1940 he had taken an apartment in villa No4 Shariah Saloh in Cairo as a bolthole; he had paid the rent for a year, and instructed his bank in Cairo to pay the next year's rent when it became due. As flamboyant as ever, he began 'cohabiting with the belly-dancer Carioca, at the time the toast of the Badia Massabni Oriental Theatre. It made a little stir.' His thinking was such an affair would cover his long absences.

On a return visit he had met his contact in the Canal Zone, Faud Osman. The latter told Eppler about some odd goings on that he had observed in a small courtyard in the city near the Groppi Tearooms. Eppler knew the owner of a house nearby, from where they could observe events unseen. Equipped with a camera they set up an observation post.

> The place looked like the backstage of a theatre or a film studio workshop. The innocent observer might have thought they were working on a war film. Four men picked up a mark VI tank and without any trouble carried it across the courtyard, loading it on to a waiting lorry. It was made of rubber. Even from as close as this, from across the street, hardly 50m away, it was indistinguishable from the real thing. They had quite a number of tanks piled up in a corner. They seemed to be mass-producing them right in the middle of a big city! Propped up against the walls of the courtyard were parachutists realistic down to the smallest detail, standing about as though having a five-minute break for a smoke! If it had not been for their height which was barely three feet, one would have taken them for real people.

This ranked amongst some of Eppler's best information obtained for his Abwehr controllers. He also learnt of deceptions to confuse aircraft.

> Camouflage and decoys seemed to be highly thought of by the British. Faud had earlier brought me material from the Canal Zone that bore this out. There they had simply covered over a part of Lake Timsah with sacking over stakes. They had painted the upper side with desert camouflage. It was superb. It was so well done, Faud had said, that it was bound to mislead any pilot and no one would be able to spot it.[6]

This may well have been the work of Jasper Maskelyne, a stage magician and illusionist, and his dedicated team, who created fake lakes to lure bombers away from Alexandria and to shield the Suez Canal. He also later created a dummy army shortly before the Battle of El Alamein. The British and to a lesser extent the Germans used this type of camouflage deception throughout the war. Perhaps the most famous dummy army deception was that assembled in East Anglia before D-Day.

In October 1940, Colonel Bonner Frank Fellers, a 1918 West Point graduate, who had been a staff officer for General Douglas MacArthur and served in the embassy in Spain, was posted to Cairo as US Military Attaché.

He kept his eyes and ears open, touring the battlefields, observing the problems and tactics of desert war. The British encouraged him, hoping to further foster friendly relations between the two countries. Fellers compiled a great quantity of information and sent it to Washington in encoded reports.[7]

Hermione, Countess of Ranfurly, working at the offices of SOE in Cairo, met Fellers in February 1941.

> Today I met Bonner Fellers, the US Military Attaché here – an original and delightful person who seems to say exactly what he thinks to everyone regardless of nationality or rank.
>
> He has just returned from the Desert and spoke with amusement and admiration of how our attack was kept secret.[8]

Fellers carefully encoded all his reports into the Black Code and sent them by radio to MILID WASH (Military Intelligence Division

Washington), signed 'Fellers'. The trouble was that Axis radio stations
– two at least – were reading every word. Within hours Rommel had
these reports, what he called '*die qute Quelle*' (the Good Source), some-
times referred to as 'the little fellows' or 'the little Fellers' reports.[9]

The Germans were able to read Fellers' messages thanks to the
actions of General Cesare Ame, head of Italy's SIM and friend of
Canaris, who had approved a break-in at the US Embassy in Rome
that September, the embassy of a still neutral country. Two of his
operatives and two Italians employed by the embassy gained access
with a set of keys that had been duplicated from the originals. They
also had keys to, and the combination of, the safe. The combination
had been provided by Loris Gherardi, a messenger in the office of the
military attaché, who had worked there since 1920.

The Black Code, so called for the colour of its cover, was
removed with the cipher tables, photographed and then replaced.
Neither Gherardi's boss, Colonel Norman E. Fiske, nor the ambassador William Phillips, ever suspected Gherardi and he continued
in his job.[10]

Count Galeazzo Ciano, son-in-law of Mussolini, wrote in his diary
on 30 September 1941 that 'the SIM have secured the American
Secret Code. Everything that Phillips cables is read by our decoding
offices …'[11] Soon after the SIM obtained the Black Code, they gave
a copy to the Abwehr. Hans-Otto Behrendt, an intelligence officer in
Rommel's HQ wrote:

> Of all the code telegrams, which included some from the US military
> attaché in Moscow, those sent by Colonel Fellers from Cairo were the
> most important; because they carried vital information on the Middle
> East battlefields. In view of the great frankness between the Americans
> and the English, this information was not only strategically but tacti-
> cally of the utmost usefulness. In fact it was stupefying in its openness.

He goes on to say that it was 'playing a role by January/February
1942' and it was so sensitive it was 'forbidden to make notes' thus
'German documents do not exist.'[12]

However examples of the information in the Fellers' signals have
been published, taken from the signals received at their intended des-
tination, Washington.

January 23; 270 airplanes and a quantity of antiaircraft artillery being withdrawn from North Africa to reinforce British forces in the Far East.

January 25–26; Allied evaluation of the defects of Axis armour and aircraft.

January 29; Complete rundown of British armour, including numbers in working order, number damaged, number available, and their locations; location and efficiency ratings of armoured and motorized units at the front.

February 1; Forthcoming commando operations; efficiency ratings of various British units; report that American M-3 tanks could not be used before mid-February.

February 6; Location and efficiency of the 4th Indian Division and the 1st Armoured Division; iteration of British plans to dig in along the Acroma-Bir Hacheim line; recognition of the possibility that Axis forces might reach the Egyptian frontier once the armoured divisions had been regrouped.[13]

Alan Moorehead, the journalist and writer, met Fellers during the Battle of Sidi Rezegh in November 1941.

My party had blundered into the British armoured division headquarters and the first officer I saw was the welcome figure of Colonel Bonner Fellers, the US Military Attache. Bonner Fellers was often in the desert. He liked to gather his facts at first hand and in the Wavell campaign we used to see him buzzing about from place to place in an ordinary civilian car.

And now, here he was again, looking quizzically across to the east where quick heavy gunfire had suddenly broken the quiet of the afternoon. I called across to him, 'What's happening?' and he just had time to reply, 'Damned if I know,' when we had to duck for shelter as two Messerschmitts came over, ground strafing.[14]

Thus the Luftwaffe unwittingly almost finished off one of Rommel's best sources of intelligence.

All this was in the future; on 5 July General Sir Claude Auchinleck took command, a 'soldier's soldier, brave, competent astute but unlucky'. This was particularly true in his choice of field commanders, resulting in him having to take the field command himself.[15]

Churchill soon began prodding and badgering Auchinleck to take the offensive; but in September the Eighth Army was formed from reinforcements and the Western Desert Force – which became XIII Corps in October – and Auchinleck explained that the army needed training and new equipment had to be properly prepared for the desert. Churchill might have reflected that he had replaced one cautious general with another. His view of warfare was more akin to that of Rommel, whom he admired.

Rommel also waited for Auchinleck, stymied by his precarious supply lines and the nagging problem of Tobruk. Eventually Auchinleck's offensive Operation *Crusader* commenced on 18 November. It had two aims: to destroy the enemy in eastern Cyrenaica and drive the enemy from Africa, which in turn would relieve Tobruk.

12. Interview with the Führer

WHEN OPERATION *CRUSADER* BEGAN, EPPLER was in Berlin. He had been summoned back almost certainly at the behest of Ritter and Canaris, who considered him an ideal candidate for placement in Egypt. Almásy had already been to Abwehr HQ to discuss 'the penetration of southern Egypt via the desert'. (British Intelligence were aware Almásy now headed the Commando in North Africa.[1]) However, Operation *Crusader* drove Rommel back to Agedabia beyond Benghazi and the Siege of Tobruk was relieved. The idea of a new operation had to be shelved.

Meanwhile the political wheels turned. Hadji Mohammed Amun el-Husseini, the Grand Mufti, had left Iran in July for Turkey, crossing the border on foot. He was soon an embarrassment to the Turks, who quickly moved him on to Italy. On 27 October he had a meeting with Mussolini, but Count Galeazzo Ciano considered him unreliable and unlikely to achieve anything.[2]

He then travelled to Germany, where he was housed in a splendid villa deep in the Zehlendorf Park. Amidst the trees and lakes of the Grunewald forest, where many Nazi officials had retreats, he was guarded by the SS. Eppler went there to visit him.

> He talked with me about his visit to Rome and his meeting with the Fascist leader, who he assured me, was eating out of his hand. There was nothing to impede the progress towards the creation of a United Arab movement with the help of Rome and Berlin.

Then he stunned Eppler with his request that he should act as his interpreter in a meeting with Hitler. He felt 'upset' yet at the same time 'attracted' by the prospect. 'Even if I distrusted Caesar, I had to admit that not everyone had the opportunity to shake his hand.'[3]

The Mufti was relieved that he agreed to the request, fearing he might have been given a German interpreter not so sympathetic to his position. He was unaware that Eppler thought him a schemer of little value.

The Mufti was kept waiting for his audience with Hitler, and Eppler kicked his heels at the Abwehr offices. On 28 November they were finally taken to the Chancellery in a huge Mercedes. Eppler recorded that it was an 'enormous building, like a pompous Roman temple – impressive and chilly'.

They waited their turn in the great hall, which was thronged with people and officials. After some time a flunky informed them they would see the Führer shortly, and then proceeded to instruct them on how to greet Hitler: 'We were to say *"Heil mein Führer"* and extend our arms horizontally, not vertically as done in Italy.'[4]

Shortly after this they were approached by Von Ribbentrop, the Foreign Minister. He told the Grand Mufti that Hitler was well briefed on the pro-Axis United Arabia. They were then searched before being led into the Führer's presence. Eppler recorded that there were four men at the meeting, including Ribbentrop, but the official minutes state there were five; Fritz Grobba – the old ambassador to Iraq and by then the foreign minister in waiting for the Arab States – was present.[5]

According to Eppler's account of the meeting, they found the room in semi-darkness; the curtains were drawn across the huge windows. Hitler was known to suffer from bouts of giddiness and light may have had some bearing on this.[6] Hitler was seated behind a desk, which he left to greet the Mufti. Eppler thought he was rather short, only having previously seen him on newsreels. He was dressed in civilian clothes and wore highly polished shoes. 'Yet his eyes were piercing and one could appreciate the hypnotic effect he had on so many people.' The Führer shook the Mufti's hand he asked if he was having a comfortable stay.[7]

It should be noted here that in the account Eppler gave of the meeting to Leonard Mosley, 'The Mufti approached the Führer and held out his hand for Hitler to shake, and then as he saw that no handshake was to be given, he drew it back and put his hand to his heart and his head, in the Arabic way, and sat down.' Eppler reminded Hitler that they had forgotten the coffee, an Arabic custom, and the Führer flew into a rage and left the room. All this seems highly unlikely and is not in Eppler's own written account; was he embellishing the story for Mosley's benefit?[8]

In Eppler's own account, Hitler, after greeting the Mufti, had turned to him shaking his hand and remarked that Arabic was 'a handsome language'. With protocol over they sat in armchairs, and the Mufti began his spiel about the Jews, Britain and Bolshevism, and how the Arabs were natural allies of the Axis powers. He stated that the Arabs wanted a declaration of friendship from Hitler and help for their cause. Eppler says he went on like this 'for at least fifteen minutes. At times I was hard pressed to translate these fiery platitudes with some degree of conviction.'

Hitler then gave his point of view, concluding that nothing could be achieved until the German armies were victorious in the great world struggle. The Grand Mufti would then become the leader of the Arabs everywhere, but until then he would not raise false hopes with a public statement.

The Mufti then suggested the drawing up of a secret treaty. Translating this Eppler felt a change in the Führer.

> He was not pleased with this. He barely listened to my last words, before he declared in an ice-cold voice that a secret agreement, treaty or declaration known to several people could not long remain secret … he had given the Mufti precisely that confidential declaration just now.

Hitler then rose, bringing the meeting to a close. He shook hands again, asking the Mufti to 'treat Germany as his own home'. He accompanied them to the doors, and they left, leaving Hitler and Ribbentrop behind.

Walking down the corridors of the Chancellery, Eppler thought: 'How much of what had been said would ever happen? How much did either of them trust the other? There had been promises and hand shaking. Was there anything else?'[9]

Part IV

KONDOR

13. Planning

ALMÁSY WAS ALSO IN BERLIN during the winter of 1941. He was clarifying his plan – Operation *Salam* – to infiltrate agents into Cairo by a 1700-mile land route, travelling via the Jalo Oasis to the Gilf Kebir plateau, bypassing the LRDG base at Kufra, east to the Kharga Oasis, then dropping the agents close to Assiut on the Nile. From there they would make their own way to Cairo where they would transmit information using the radios they brought with them to 'Abteilung I attached to the headquarters of the Panzer Armee in Africa'.[1] Once the agents were on their own in Cairo, the transmission of intelligence would come under the codename of Operation *Kondor*.

But which agents should be sent to Cairo? They would have to be resourceful men. Eppler was one. He claimed to have known Almásy before the war, even accompanying him on one of his trips into the desert.

> The assurance of the man Almásy was truly enviable. He had not changed since the day in 1935, we had broken down with engine trouble near the great Mohariq Barkan Dune. We had been searching for the lost oasis and were resigned to awaiting the end, but he quite calmly repeated; 'The last moment has not yet come. Someone will turn up and get us out of this.' And right enough, someone did just about at curtain time. It was Robert Clayton, who took us back to the Nile Valley.[2]

Eppler indicates that he met Almásy again in May 1942; other sources say they met in Vienna in the autumn of 1941 to discuss the mission.[3]

Hans Gerd Sandstette was the other agent (known as Sandy by Eppler and Sandstette to British intelligence.)[4] He was born in Oldenburg in 1913 and lived in Germany until 1930 when he immigrated to West Africa, going on to work in several parts of the continent. He was arrested and interned by the British in Dar-es-Salaam, but was repatriated to Germany in January 1940 in a British-German exchange of civilians. Like Eppler, he came under the wing of the Abwehr, and worked in the Army Topographical Department on maps. He was given a forged British passport in the name of Peter Muncaster – an American he had met in East Africa – to be used once in Cairo (Operation *Kondor*). Although Sandy became known as Eppler's 'expert radio operator', both men underwent W/T training, first in Munich and then at the Abwehr wireless station at Berlin-Stansdorf.[5]

In December 1941 Almásy left for Africa. In mid-February 1942 the rest of the party followed, leaving Berlin by train. Comprising Eppler, Sandy and three wireless operators under Sergeant Major Hans Von Steffens, they took with them specialist equipment, sand ladders and radio sets modified for the desert.

The British were reading the Abwehr messages, albeit with a fairly low priority as far as the 'Almásy Commando' was concerned. On 20 February they knew Von Steffens' party had 'left for Rome on 18 February', that they were cleared to use 'the air route' to Tripoli for 'Max and Moritz' and had been ordered to 'inform Almásy of this'.[6]

Max and Moritz were Sandy and Eppler's codenames. Both had left in such a hurry they had not paid bills left in their lodgings, and Almásy received a message from Abwehr HQ, asking him to deduct these costs from their wages, an unusual use of a supposedly secure radio link.[7]

Arriving in Naples they flew on to Tripoli in Luftwaffe JU 52 transport planes. In Tripoli they spent time overhauling their British trucks – 0.5-ton Ford V8s and 1.5-ton Bedford lorries – for the desert journey. They were fitted with light machine guns and the three Fords carried Ascania global compasses. The command vehicle also carried a sextant. All vehicles were marked with German crosses – in accordance with the Geneva Convention – but were sprayed with sand so these could only be seen at close quarters. From the air they would appear British. All personnel wore German uniforms to prevent them being shot if captured.

During this time, the spring of 1942, Almásy's name came to the attention of Jean Howard, then Miss Jean Alington, a young linguist working at Bletchley Park's Hut 3. This was the sorting hut for Hut 6 – a decoding hut – which passed messages to Hut 3 for translation, analysis and dispatch.[8] Miss Alington noticed some Abwehr intercepts relating to the 'Almásy Commando', which seemed to have been overlooked. It is not surprising that a rather obscure Hungarian was considered of little importance given the volume of work; the Battle of the Atlantic was raging and other resources were concentrated on Rommel's next offensive in the desert war. However, she noted that the codename *Salam* seemed to relate to an operation. 'I had noticed this Almásy Commando was to go through a part of North Africa [near the Qattara Depression] where we had a false army, a signal unit, not tanks etc., but signals being sent out to look as though it was an entire army.' She sought and was given permission from her superiors to keep an eye on Almásy, providing she did it in her own time.

Jean felt that 'this man must be caught.' She later revealed in an interview her anxiety:

> It would be terrible if we didn't send someone to catch him before he discovered the truth about our phantom army. So I got permission to send a message to Cairo that aircraft should fly from Kufra Oasis to look for him and alternatively that we should send people up from the south to do what they could, but to pick them up alive. It seemed to me very important not to kill them but to pick them up alive.

Her rather precautionary tone here reflects the need above all to protect Ultra.[9]

The situation in Africa when Eppler and his companions arrived in Tripoli in February 1942 had been shaped by the military events during and following Operation *Crusader*. Auchinleck's winter offensive – launched in November 1941 – had caught Rommel unprepared; the General had to hurry back from Rome, where he had been on leave. On the 17th the British had launched a preparatory commando raid against what they thought to be Rommel's headquarters at Beda Littoria, hoping to kill or capture him. By that time it was HQ of the Quartermaster-General Major Schleusener. Rommel had not used it for months, a fact which British intelligence had failed to pick up. Even though the attacking commandos pressed home the attack with great courage, it was a fruitless undertaking. Even Schleusener was not in the HQ; he was in hospital at Apollonia having gone down with dysentery. Only a few staff officers and other ranks were present.[10]

In the six weeks of confused fighting that followed, the British relieved Tobruk and pushed the Axis forces back 400 miles. Rommel's leadership and superior armour were unable to save the situation, for he was hamstrung by his supply lines. Thanks partly to Ultra, the Royal Navy and RAF operating largely from Malta were able to sink fourteen of the 22 ships sent to Africa over this period. Rommel was defeated, not by superior force or superior generalship but by lack of materiel.

The Eighth Army hardly looked like a victorious force; hundreds of its burnt-out tanks and vehicles littered the desert. Auchinleck even had to relieve its leader, Lieutenant-General Cunningham, of his command during the battle, as the man was exhausted and on the verge of a nervous breakdown. Major-General Neil Ritchie, Deputy Chief of Staff at GHQ, took over. He was extremely reluctant to do so believing he was only qualified to command a Corps but Auchinleck felt that Ritchie had the drive and boldness Cunningham lacked. He was right in this, but so was Ritchie in saying that he lacked the experience to handle such a large force and complex battle. He failed to raise confidence in his officers or morale in his men; the latter had an unbounded admiration for Rommel.

The pendulum of the desert war was already swinging back toward the Axis. Japan's entry into the war in December meant reinforcements for the desert were diverted to India and Malaya. However unlike during the Greek fiasco of 1941, the Eighth Army was not stripped of men or equipment.

Eventually Rommel's supply situation improved; ships started to get through in larger numbers as Malta was pounded by the Luftwaffe, and the Royal Navy suffered one of its worst periods of the war. *Repulse* and *Prince of Wales* were lost off Malaya, *Ark Royal* and *Barham* were sunk by U-boats in the Mediterranean and *Valiant* and *Queen Elizabeth* were sunk by Italian 'human torpedoes' in Alexandria harbour (although both would be salvaged and return to the fight). In Egypt King Farouk was said to have celebrated the sinking of the aircraft carrier *Ark Royal* with a glass of champagne.[11]

'On 21 January' Auchinleck reported 'the improbable occurred, and without warning the Axis forces began to advance.' Taken by surprise by the re-supplied and regrouped Afrika Korps, the battle raced back eastward. Benghazi and Derna were reoccupied.

Rommel's drive came to a halt on 7 February on a line running south from Gazala, 100 miles east along the Via Balbia from Derna. A three-month lull descended on the desert war.[12]

The Almásy Commando remained in Tripoli, having no direct role to perform, awaiting personnel and equipment. But Operation *Salam* was very much a go.

14. The Rebecca Code

On 10 April British Intelligence noted that Admiral Canaris – the 'Berlin Gentleman' – was touring his 'nests' in Libya and Tunis.[1] A few days before this, Almásy was moving up to a forward position; he hoped to have everything ready for Operation *Salam* in nine or ten days. He had to dodge the RAF attacks on traffic along the Via Balbia, quickly getting off the road into cover at the sight of any aircraft. About 450 miles east of Tripoli he almost drove into a sand dune in a frantic attempt to conceal his vehicle.

> The plane comes like an arrow from hell, skimming a few metres above the highway. The pilot really knows his business, even taking advantage of the line of little sand dunes. Once or twice he disappears below the outline of dunes, occasionally barking out a machine gun volley. Far ahead black smoke is rising; he's already caused some damage. He'll be on us in seconds.
>
> I can make out his profile for an instant behind the windshield. Suddenly a sub-machine gun is fired right next to me. The radio operator is standing there with legs akimbo, blasting away at the enemy plane …[2]

A few miles further east he came across Italian trucks on fire, having been strafed by the RAF, with several of the crew dead and wounded. 'This was an ugly business, hunting down vehicles on the highway.'[3]

Passing through Agedabia near Benghazi, he recalled happier times:

> My comrades and Italian friends think it's the most desolate, boring, and despicable nest in all Libya. It's true that the entire town consists of only four streets and that the number of trees can be counted on two hands, but here, hidden behind high walls, is the former palace of my friend Sayed Idris, the Great Sanusi. The interior of the building evokes the atmosphere of the *Thousand and One Nights*. With a heavy heart, I realise that this unfortunate war has probably extinguished forever the romantic allure of Libya, and that the days may never return when we

When on leave in Cairo the Pyramids were a must to visit, at least for these Royal Navy nurses. Second from the left is the author's aunt. (Olive Hard Collection)

Cairo White Domes of the Mohammed Ali Mosque at the Citadel. (Olive Hard Collection)

The Kharga Oasis, used by both the Allied and Axis forces during the war.

n Egyptian snake charmer. (Olive Hard Collection)

dmiral Wilhelm Canaris, head of
e Abwehr. (Akg-images)

An Italian Auto-Saharan desert patrol. (Revista Militar Italy)

László Almásy and Nickolaus Ritter planning a desert operation.

The Grand Mufti, Hadji Mohammed Amin el Husseini, in Berlin.

Major A.W. Sansom, head of British Field Security, Cairo.

Heinrich Gerd Sandstette and Johannes Eppler before they set off on Operation *Salam*.

The Egyptian Sand Sea. (Almásy Hungarian National Geographic Centre)

Cave paintings at the Gilf Kebir. (Almásy Hungarian National Geographic Centre)

The Gilf Kebir from the air.

The Gilf Kebir plateau. (Almásy Hungarian National Geographic Centre)

Almásy at a road sign near Assiut, taken before dropping
Eppler and Sandstette off in the desert. (Revista Militar Italy)

Eppler in Cairo, 1942, dressed in the uniform of an officer of the Rifle Brigade.

Likely cover of the *Rebecca* edition used in Operation *Kondor*. (Bookends of Fowey)

Rommel the Desert Fox; always up with the action, here in winter 1941. (US National Archives)

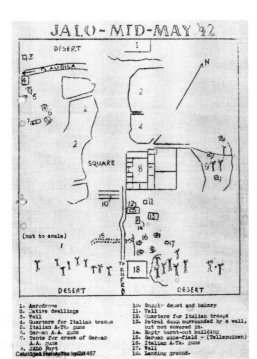

JALO - MID - MAY '42

DESERT

SQUARE

(not to scale)

DESERT   DESERT

1. Aerodrome
2. Native dwellings
3. Well
4. Quarters for Italian troops
5. Italian A-Tk. guns
6. German A-A. guns
7. Tents for crews of German A.A. guns
a. JALO Fort
10. Supply depot and bakery
11. Well
12. Quarters for Italian troops
13. Petrol dump surrounded by a wall, but not covered in.
14. Empty burnt-out building
15. German mine-field - (Tellerminen)
16. Italian A-Tk. guns
17. Well
18. Landing ground.

The Jalo Oasis and Axis camp, drawn by Eppler under interrogation. (Public Records Office)

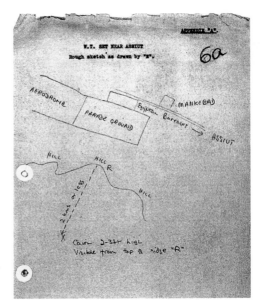

The burial site of equipment near Assiut, drawn by Eppler under interrogation. (Public Records Office)

Anti-aircraft fire over the desert near a field hospital. (Olive Hard Collection)

General Bernard Law Montgomery, the Eighth Army commander, with General Dempsey, Brigadier Hayman-Joyce and Major Sansom, shown here leaving GHQ Cairo.

Montgomery on the move. (US National Archives)

Nickolaus Ritter. seen here in Hamburg after the war, while he was working for the CIA.

ppler and the biographer Leonard
Mosley in discussion.

The bust of László Almásy at the Hungarian Geographical
Museum in Érd. (Hungarian National Geographic Centre)

could sit on colourful rugs in dusky chambers with pointed arches, slurping tea flavoured with mint essence of rose.[4]

Little did he realise that one day his own name would add to the 'romantic allure' of the desert.

His night near Benghazi was not a very restful one, as the RAF bombed the town. 'I burrowed into the ground and tried to make my head disappear between my shoulders at the hateful, ghastly whoosh of incoming bombs ...'[5]

The next day Almásy learnt that one of his men, Hans Entholt, had been injured in an air attack whilst travelling in another vehicle. He referred to him as his 'officer candidate', and had known him before the war. The two men had met in 1938, when Entholt was working as an actor. They had drifted apart in 1939 when Hans was called up for the army. Some suspected that the two men were romantically involved; the late John Bierman certainly thought so: 'This man was, in fact, Almásy's pre-war lover, Hans Entholt. Almásy had managed to get him switched to North Africa from a posting to the Russian front, the pair obviously having become reconciled ...'[6]

It does seem odd that Almásy should request Entholt to join his command as a medical orderly.

He's an old friend and I requested his reassignment to my unit. We haven't seen each other in a long time and my young German friend has experienced a great deal ... He has fought in the Polish and French campaigns and upon learning that I was on the African front, he badgered me to get him reassigned. Being in charge of a special detachment, I was entitled to select personally the members of the unit, but I was reluctant to place a young man's life at risk under my command.[7]

Almásy rushed off to the crowded field hospital where he found his friend had his head bandaged. However he was put at ease when he was greeted with a big smile and when Entholt asked 'permission to leave here immediately'. Almásy concluded that 'It's not so easy to crack one of these German skulls.'[8]

The Almásy group had to stay in Benghazi for a few days, close to Rommel's field headquarters, where they waited for a final briefing with Rommel and Canaris. Eppler, Sandy and Almásy were in the briefing room before the high ranking officers arrived. Canaris shambled in first. He was not in uniform, but wore 'a cheap jacket he had bought in Madrid' with a pair of 'shabby unpressed grey flannel trousers'. He revelled in wearing disguises, perhaps a throw-back to his earlier life as a spy.[9] Rommel was rather different as he rushed in, full of purpose, straight from the front line. 'He's wearing a long cloak as protection against the dust, a light colourful scarf and an officer's cap, with goggles perched on top.'[10] He was sweating in his regulation field grey uniform, and had desert sores on his lips.

He told the assembled Almásy Commando that their mission was critical to his drive to the Suez Canal and to take Cairo, for they might not get another chance. He told Eppler and Sandy: 'We need information about the enemy's intentions, I need another network in Cairo.' He paused for a comment from Canaris, but the Admiral remained silent.

'In the next few weeks I need a totally reliable unit in Egypt. It is absolutely essential. I don't want a second failure like that business with the aeroplane.' He may have indicated too that it was unwise to rely on the 'Good Source' indefinitely (the intercepted reports written by the American Colonel Bonner Frank Fellers).[11] Almásy knew about this intelligence:

> This source can dry up. No military leader can tolerate a constant leakage of news to the enemy for any length of time. A trifling mistake, an indiscretion, a piece of treachery and the source will be closed.[12]

Canaris now spoke, indicating there were no guarantees in such operations, but the men were the best he had. All had 'spent years in the Orient.' Rommel seemed happy with this and turned to Almásy.

'It's a bold plan, I hope you don't die in the damned desert.' Almásy pointed out his experience and said that the desert held no fears for him.

'Oh well,' said Rommel 'they say lunatics are usually lucky. Why shouldn't you be?'[13]

Rommel left. 'The meeting lasted just a few minutes, but I again felt the spell that Rommel cast on his troops.'[14]

A novel was to play a key role in the work of the Almásy Commando: Daphne du Maurier's *Rebecca*. One wonders if Canaris, having come to Africa via Spain, had brought copies of *Rebecca* with him; the wife of the German assistant military attaché in Portugal had purchased six copies of the novel only days before at an English-language book shop in Estoril on 3 April. Some sources indicate Eppler already had a copy when he left for North Africa in February but this would seem unlikely.[15]

Rebecca was published in 1938, at 384 pages, with a first impression cheap edition print run of 20,000 copies; the tenth impression was published in July 1939. Neville Chamberlain had gone to Munich in September 1938, carrying a copy in his briefcase for relaxation between his meetings with Hitler.[16] *Rebecca* sold a million copies in the first year of publication and in two decades ran to 39 impressions. In Cairo, the film version had been running for many months since its release in 1940; directed by Alfred Hitchcock, it starred Laurence Olivier and Joan Fontaine, who was almost unknown before being nominated for an Oscar for her performance as Du Maurier's heroine.

The novel had a distinct Victor Gollancz yellow cover with red and black lettering, the author's name in black, the title in red, and early editions had the strapline 'new novel' in black italics between. By 1941 it ran from the 21st impression to the 27th, and 'new novel' had been replaced by 'the famous bestseller'; it is more than likely that the *Kondor* books would have been one of these, some of which had the price on the cover of 4/6d.[17] The Portuguese bookseller had marked the inside of his copies with his own price, 50 escudos, which the Germans half-heartedly tried to remove.

Rebecca was to be used as a code book by the agents. Using the book, or any book, as a code was fairly straightforward. Sentences were made using single words in the book, referred to by page numbers, line and position in the line. Page numbers changed every day. It was a secure method of communication so long as no one else knew the title of the de-code manual, or book.

15. False Start

OPERATION *SALAM* – THE JOURNEY across the desert to Cairo – did not begin until 29 April. On 7 April Bletchley Park deciphered a message from Almásy dated 27 March that revealed they would be ready in '9 or 10 days' and he would 'arrive at the forward position in my own car on Monday or Tuesday.' The forward position was the Jalo Oasis.[1]

Eppler says he rode with Almásy to Jalo from Benghazi; 'Almásy sat next to me as we drove, smoking a cigarette.' Once at Jalo 'we would prepare oursselves for the journey itself. We would check our supplies and vehicles and stock up with water before pushing on into the desert.'[2]

Jalo was not the cool oasis they had hoped. Eppler found it lacked 'purling brooks there, no wonderfully scented fruit and no mysterious black female eyes. In fact, there was no romance to be found there at all.' As for the oasis, 'the springs are brackish and the inhabitants surly. A thousand palm trees and filthy mud huts stood in a hollow in the middle of the desert. The wind blows ceaselessly; there is never an end to it.'[3]

All the same he was glad to get there, even if confused about the date. Eppler states they arrived at Jalo on 11 May but this is clearly a mistake in his account.

> As our column drove into the oasis, the soldiers of the small Italian garrison were sitting listlessly chatting about their girlfriends back home. We exchanged greetings in a desultory way. Our limbs were leaden and our brains numb. We needed a long break.[4]

Almásy found the oasis and the Italians rather different.

> Besides the padre, I'm the only guest in the officer's mess of the small fort. The Italians – some 30 infantry officers of different ranks and ages – are all from the same division. They've been here without rotation or leave since the reoccupation of the Oasis some three months ago, and are a good natured bunch.[5]

The padre had come to celebrate Easter Sunday Mass. They enjoyed a special meal to which Almásy and his men were invited. Even the weather improved: 'A pleasant northern breeze is blowing.' They dined on rice soup and roast lamb, and 'pastry with a genuine fruit taste is served. Cyrenaica red wine helps to create the excellent mood.' The Italians began the inevitable sing-song. 'Many evenings I had heard them singing their gorgeous tunes in beautiful tenor, baritone, and bass voices. Today's program consists mostly of marches ... and the inevitable "Lili Marlene" with four voices as always.' By this time Rommel had asked Radio Belgrade – which broadcast to German troops – to play 'Lili Marlene' every day. They could not ignore his request, and the song became the sign-off number at 9:55pm, and was quickly taken up by all the desert armies.[6]

Two British Beaufighters spoiled the festivities at the oasis by carrying out a strafing run. One man of the garrison was killed and two wounded; the Almásy group helped throw up a curtain of anti-aircraft fire. Both aircraft were damaged, forcing them to crash land in the desert; a garrison soldier on the airfield perimeter saw one of the aircraft losing height, and marked the direction. Almásy took a reading on the bearing with his prismatic compass, and in the morning a patrol set out on that bearing to take a look.

> We had only gone 10 kilometres when something suddenly loomed on the eastern horizon. Even on the hard-surfaced sand it's not advisable to brake forcefully. The tyres can sink through the hard upper crust, leaving the car bottomed out. I step off the gas, wait until the car rolls to a stop, and then climb on the roof. The silhouette of the grounded enemy airplane is clearly visible through the field glasses.

They approached the aircraft cautiously, finally finding that the crew had set out on foot. Jalo was only eight miles away, but that way lay captivity. Some 30 miles to the northwest was another small oasis, and Almásy concluded that the crew must have gone there, a place only occasionally visited by Italian patrols. They followed the British tracks, which were fairly straight, implying that the men had a compass.

> It's a weird sensation, moving across the endless flat surface, heading towards the horizon without a single reference point. I drive slowly,

> not wanting to lose the footprints weaving gently in front of us. Here
> the desert is like a tennis court without bounds, smooth as a tabletop
> and without a single pebble on the reddish yellow surface.

Within an hour they reached the oasis, where the Arab children confirmed the presence of 'inglesi'. The two RAF men were exhausted
by the desert hike, 'their footwear shredded by the abrasive sand.'
They offered no resistance and were 'somewhat stunned that we
[were there] so soon'.[7]

Almásy's presence at the Easter Day celebrations places him at Jalo
by 5 April 1942. On 14 April, Almásy requested the Abwehr commis-
sary in Berlin 'send 3 cases of tobacco in paper. I should like to leave
on the 20th.'[8]

Up until this point Bletchley Park had been able to decipher communications between Berlin and the Almásy Commando, but then
could intercept nothing until 25 May. This was mainly due to the fact
that once Almásy set off, all communications switched to a local radio
network in Libya, not via Tripoli and on to Berlin. Also, Bletchley
Park was extremely busy in this period; as we have seen, Almásy was
given a low priority until Jean Alington alerted MI6 to his activities.[9]

Why was there such a delay in setting off from Jalo? No doubt
Almásy wanted his men to get used to the vehicles and driving in the
terrain. In addition, Rommel's main advance east from Benghazi –
resulting in the Gazala battles – did not begin until 26 May.

On 29 April they set off and quickly realised that the Italian maps
were inaccurate; these stated that there was *serir* (gravel as hard as concrete on which vehicles could travel quickly) as far as the Dukhla Oasis,
Almásy's chosen route. But 30 miles east of the Palificata Track the commandos encountered dunes, which could only be crossed by zigzagging,
a time- and fuel-consuming technique. In two days they covered only
20 miles, all in 120-degree daytime heat, and freezing nights.

On the third day Entholt, who was known as the 'junior doctor',
succumbed to desert colic, an illness caused by exhaustion, resulting
in loss of balance and fainting fits. There was no remedy other than
rest. Then Von Steffen, the Sergeant Major, fell ill. He, after Almásy,
was the main driving force of the unit: 'He had been the genius of
the technical side of Operation *Salam*.' It was Von Steffen who had
found out from a local that the water from the Jalo wells would not

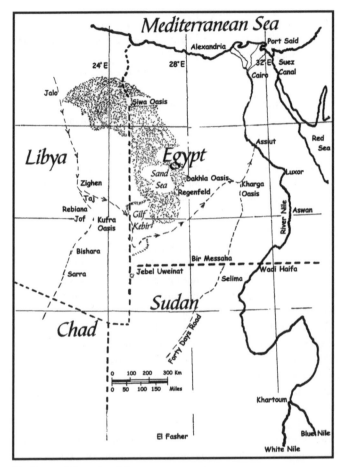

The Route of Operation *Salam*.

keep and would be undrinkable within three days, and they had had
to obtain fresh water at Bir Butafall a dozen miles away. There was
no choice, with two men seriously ill, they had to turn back to Jalo.[10]

They were back at Jalo by 6 May where Almásy had no alternative
but to send both invalids back to Tripoli for treatment. The British
were wrongly led to believe that Sergeant Von Steffens had returned
to Tripoli to become CSM of another expedition.[11] Later both
Entholt and Von Steffens were sent to a military hospital in Germany.

On 8 May Almásy conducted an air reconnaissance from Jalo to find a new route: 'If the entire zone is impassable I shall travel via Kufra through territory known to me.'[12]

The Almásy Commando set out once again on 11 May.

> It was 5 o'clock and the night was visibly clearing over the endless sand plain to the west. It was cold, bitterly cold. The bonnets of our vehicles were drawn abreast and pointing south. The needles of their Askania gyro-compasses had been checked against each other. Their steering had been tightened. We were waiting for the command to go. Fingers stiff with cold were warmed for the last time round hot tin tea mugs, from which we took short sips. Seconds later we were streaking over the surface of the *serir*, baked hard over millions of years.[13]

Having made a camp 170 miles south of Jalo, Almásy was however forced to consider taking a longer but less punishing route. He radioed back to Jalo on 13 May, reporting that one car was abandoned due to a damaged gear box, and stating that the 'dune region east of Gialo–Kufra track [was] impassible.'[14]

He decided to take the route via Kufra and the Gilf Kebir and on to Assiut; however, this meant a complete recalculation, as it was a detour of 300 miles in both directions, increasing the distance to a round trip of over 2000 miles. It was risky, as Kufra was in British hands, but he decided 'We must go via Kufra, the task must be carried out.'[15]

Vehicle and personnel numbers would have to be reduced in order to stretch the fuel and water, so two men and a Bedford truck were sent back to Jalo. Four vehicles would go on, two Ford V8s and two Bedfords. Those travelling with Almásy would be Eppler and Sandstette, and three Brandenburg corporals: Munz, Woehrmann and Koerper. They set out once again on 15 May.

Left behind at Jalo – specifically the Italian W/T station codenamed '*Schildkroete*' (Tortoise) – was the W/T operator Lance Corporal Waldemar Weber, *Salam*'s link to Rommel. His operator code was Otter. He reported directly to Abteilung I, a small unit of six junior officers attached to the mobile HQ of Panzerarmee Afrika under G2 (Intelligence) Major Ernst Zalling.[16] *Salam* traffic with Schildkroete was to report daily at 0900, 1500 or 2030hrs.[17]

16. Operation *Salam*

THE ALMÁSY COMMANDO SET OFF once again at 08:30 on 15 May. They headed south along the Palificata Track as far as KM 410 without seeing any trace of the British. Then they struck the edge of the dune country, skirting the vast Rebiana Sand Sea to the west.

For the purposes of W/T transmission, Almásy codenamed Eppler and Sandstette 'Pit' and 'Pan'. He was not overly impressed by them, and makes no mention of having known Eppler before the war, as stated by Eppler. Both agents were nervous about his plan to take the Kufra Route, fearing an encounter with the enemy.[1] Almásy found their personal organisation sorely lacking. They were 'the most untidy fellows I've ever had under me. The inside of the radio car looks frightful, loads, personal effects, weapons and food all mixed up.'[2] Almásy was not keen on his Brandenburg corporals either, as they lacked experience. None of them, despite Eppler's supposed knowledge of the desert, had much experience that could assist him.

Almásy radioed in on 15 May indicating that they were setting off and 'according to a recce the British post is supposed to be near Br Abu Zereigh. I shall attempt to turn SW before then.'[3] It was at this point that radio communication between Otter at Jalo and *Salam* broke down. The culprit was Schildkroete itself (the Italian W/T station at Jalo) and the Italian W/T stations on the oasis. Interference from them was so bad that they had to take over the link to *Salam*, passing messages on to Otter. To make matters worse the Abwehr W/T station in Athens, codenamed 'Adolf', was largely kept in the dark; it seems unlikely that they had the right copy of *Rebecca* to decode *Salam*'s messages, or even the German work, an edition from the Leipzig-based publisher Bernard Tauchnitz, which was being used by all W/T stations for encoding.[4]

Four hours after setting off, the Almásy Commando passed near the British post to the north of Kufra Oasis. By this time it was noon; the timing was intentional as Almásy thought that 'Tommy' would be sleeping during the hottest part of the day. Then at about 15:00 'Pan' got 'Maria' – one of the Bedford trucks – stuck in soft sand. It took them two hours to get it out.

Not long afterwards Almásy found 'traces of the old Trucchi Track from the years 1932–33. At that time the Palificata did not exist and the heavy diesel trucks made a way through the hills with their double tyres. It is easy to keep to the track.'[5] At 19:00 they stopped for the night, having covered 130 miles. Almásy hid four cans of petrol and two cans of water behind a crag for the return journey.

The next day they set off at 06:00 along the Trucchi Track, the 'smugglers road' past the danger zone of Kufra and due east of Jof, the main village of the Kufra Oasis. Almásy came across fresh tracks of more than 100 trucks. They could only be from British vehicles, and he was surprised: 'I had no idea that enemy columns were running from the east toward Kufra.' He changed course to follow the tracks; 'Duney sand, heavy going. Tommy has also ploughed in deeply and often stuck.' He thought the British might have used it only a few hours previously.

By the end of the day they had covered another 155 miles. They camped in the saddle between two hills and left another small supply dump, six cans of petrol, one can of water and a case of rations. Almásy wanted to radio a report but Woehrmann could not raise either Otter or Schildkroete.[6]

They left at 06:40 the next morning, 17 May. Almásy looked for his old route between Kufra and the Gilf Kebir plateau on the bearing 122, finding the Italian maps of little help, as they failed to show a range of hills that barred their way. This meant a detour south, where they came across the tracks of hundreds of vehicles and two abandoned Sudan Defence Force trucks, the odometer of one showing 433 miles. It was now obvious that Kufra was not supplied from the south, from French territory as previously thought, but rather from further north from Wadi Haifa and the head of the Sudan railway.

The going began to get very hard.

> Dissected plateaux, soft shifting sand, tail dunes of the 'giras' sand hills',
> he continually has to change course and bearings. Woehrmann is of
> little help, he ... is not capable of reckoning bearings and distances
> for me. I am constantly forced to stop and to check the courses on the
> useless Italian map.[7]

Almásy found the way onto a stony plain of shale and suddenly the surface was much better; 'At last we had good going again, and could make up for lost time.'[8]

However, it was clear that enemy vehicles were using the same route, so while the going was much better the men had to be cautious. Almásy soon spotted tell-tale clouds of dust ahead so they turned off the track and concealed the vehicles behind rocks. Climbing onto the roof of one of them, Almásy looked through binoculars and counted five dust plumes, five trucks, concluding that they 'must drive carefully in order not to overtake the Tommy column inadvertently.' Luck was on their side, as he also managed to see the outline of Gilf Kebir plateau on the eastern horizon, a familiar landmark. Within a few miles he would be able to use his own maps.

They drove through a narrow defile, and between two jutting white rocks Almásy called 'the Gateway to Egypt' the 'el Bab el Misr'. At last 'everything was familiar to me ... Allahu Akhbar [God is great].'[9]

Soon the ground was red and sandy heading toward the Gilf Kebir; the tell-tale plumes of the British vehicles disappeared. At 18:30 they stopped for the night, hiding in the foothills of the Gilf. More supplies were unloaded for the return journey: six cans of petrol, three cans of water and a day's ration for four men.

It was all a great strain on Almásy.

> At night, my eyes burn painfully, and even when they're closed I continue to see the compass needle, with the numbers dancing in the background. Who knows how many hundreds of kilometres we've driven, how many tracks we've crossed, how often tense watchfulness has succumbed to utter exhaustion. Driving, nonstop driving, always following the enemy tracks.
>
> When the sun finally dips below the horizon and we stop in a favourite hideout, my men first set up a camp bed next to my car so that I can stretch out on it, with a cold compress over my eyes. This is my only privilege, and they insist on it. They know that I'm the most exhausted, with eyes burning from constantly staring at the compass.[10]

He also suffered bad bouts of insomnia.

Eppler was well aware how Almásy felt even without the strain of using the compass in the heat and glare.

No one wanted anything to eat. We had even almost forgotten our thirst. Hardly had the monotonous roar of the engines fallen silent than we lay down, just as we got out of the vehicles, right between them, utterly worn out. We pulled the blankets over our heads and slept as if we had died till daybreak.[11]

The next day they left one of the Bedfords at their camp, painting out the identification German crosses and removing everything that might give a clue to their mission. Almásy left a note in French, stating that the vehicle would be picked up when they 'return from Kufra'. It was hoped that if the British found the vehicle they would think it was French.

The supplies were redistributed amongst the three remaining vehicles and the convoy set off at 09:25. They soon reached the Wadi Sura (the Valley of the Swimmers) a place familiar to Almásy, as it had made his reputation as an explorer. Nine years before he had discovered its cave paintings, and he showed these to his *Salam* companions.

Ten years earlier Almásy had sought and found the Oasis of the Little Birds, the 'Zarsura', in the Gilf Kebir. Together with the Englishman Clayton, who was knocking around not far from us as our enemy [by this time Clayton was in a POW camp in Italy], they had travelled down the Wadi Hamra and had found a hidden valley in the south, amid the high crags of the Gilf, which could only be the 'Zarsura' …

It was supposed to have been as green as the Garden of Eden and full of antelopes and gazelles. It was said to have been inhabited by thousands of small birds and to have had water. Above all water, any amount of it, flowing down the wadi.[12]

Further on they came across the three distinct craggy peaks of the Drei Burgen (Three Castles). Here Almásy had left a water store in 1932, topping it up in 1933, in a cave on the eastern 'castle'.

There were eight cans. This store had saved the life of Almásy's pre-war friend Ralph Bagnold in 1935, when the truck he and a companion were driving had broken down. The men of Operation *Salam* found that four of the tin cans had rusted through, but four were intact, and they found the water 'excellent.'[13] Eppler testified to this as he had a 'canister of Nile water tipped over [his] head'. Almásy had promised to pour one over his 'fat head'.[14]

From the heights Almásy spotted a group of parked enemy vehicles in the plain below, an area he had used as a landing strip in the 1930s. He watched them for a while but saw no sign of movement. He and Corporal Munz drove down in a Ford to take a look, and found six trucks of the Sudan Defence Force seemingly abandoned. The vehicles were laden with empty fuel drums, but the trucks' fuel tanks were full, presumably left to be picked up on some return journey. Almásy realised that with this fuel he could easily reach his objective with the two Fords and even pick up one of the Bedfords on the way back. He would not have to worry about air re-supply, which was becoming a concern as radio contact was distinctly unreliable.

He signalled the rest of the team to come down and together they drained the fuel tanks into empty drums and loaded them onto the Bedford, some 500 litres (110 gallons) in all. They then incapacitated the enemy trucks by putting sand in the engines, taking care to leave no trace of sand around the oil filler caps. They left camp and travelled northeast, hiding the stolen fuel amongst some black rocks, 'so that none could be seen, even from vehicles that might follow our tracks.'[15]

At last Woehrmann managed to raise Schildkroete and reported that they had reached the Gilf Kebir on 18 May. 'Tortoise' passed this on to Abteilung I at Panzerarmee Afrika, who responded that *Salam*'s messages were hard to read: 'Please inform *Salam*'s W/T operator that his "handwriting" shows room for improvement.' Was this rebuke intended for *Salam* or Schildkroete or both?[16]

On 19 May they set off at 07:15. Almásy had some difficulty finding the entrance to El Aqaba, which had been obscured through overuse by the British. After taking a new bearing he found the outlet of the Wadi, but he was worried that the British might have mined it.

For a moment I am beset by fear, perhaps they have mined the pass from above downwards or blown it up at its narrowest point. There was talk of that in 1937; I even had to give an opinion as to whether it was feasible.

I drive in front and look for traces of mines, but on reaching the top I find the solution to the puzzle. A number of enemy vehicles did indeed, about a year ago, drive down the great rift in the Gilf Kebir but did not find the entrance to the pass even up above and went down into the plain through 'Penderel's Wadi' which is E of El Aqaba. Penderel's Wadi is impassably low; it is a steep ravine with many twists and soft drifting sand. The English must have done some fine swearing.[17]

It was a bad day, as a spring broke on Almásy's vehicle and they covered only 50 miles. The next day had better prospects, as Almásy found his old tracks and followed them, reaching the north point of the Gilf Kebir and then turning southeast. He had discovered the pass seven years before, and by keeping to his old route he got his men over the tail-dune that blocked the pass. The men under his command were a continual cause of irritation.

> Pit as usual drives like a wild man and instead of following any track he drives 'the President' [one of the Fords] head over heels down over the steep part of the tail-dune. A miracle that the vehicle does not overturn at the bottom. Result: broken track-rod on the shock absorber.[18]

They stopped for the night at Zwei Bruste (Two Breasts) on the plain close to the eastern slope of the Gilf Kebir. Their usual habit was to park for the night in a staggered fashion, facing the wind, far enough apart so that if a fire broke out it would not spread rapidly. Fire was the greatest threat, there being fuel everywhere, in the vehicles, in cans, in the open primus stoves they cooked on.

> One must be extremely cautious around the gas cans, which are always condensing. If we spend more than one night at the same spot, we unload the gas cans and place them beyond the reach of any wind-swept sparks.[19]

They set off again at 06:30 on 21 May, leaving behind another store of fuel and water. It was difficult country, the most difficult so far.

> Low plateaus and over and over again small hills with the tail-dunes which are such a nuisance, broad plains with shale stretches and only now and again a piece of open *serir.* The vehicles suffer terribly on this kind of ground ...[20]

Progress was slow to the area south of the Dakhla Oasis. There they left 'Flitzer' (the last of the Bedfords) at a mountain with two peaks, along with some fuel and water. According to Eppler, 'Flitzer got irretrievably stuck in a fissure of rock on the Gilf. We were bound to lose one somewhere along the way. For all I know, it's there to this day.' They were in fact well past the Gilf Kebir by this time. Almásy does not mention this; would they have left fuel and water with a damaged vehicle?

Eppler found the journey arduous and hair-raising at times.

Most of the time on the way up to the Plateau the right wheel of the car was using only half the width of the tread. The other half was turning on air over a sheer drop of several hundred metres.[21]

They followed Ralph Bagnold's mapped route part of the way, and Almásy ordered an early camp; the strain was starting to tell. 'While I rest my eyes, the others perform the evening chores.'[22] In fact he had little rest, as he was once again frustrated by his men, this time over communications. He found he had to repair the radio transformer himself: 'Three radio-operators and a mechanic are not in a position to find out what is wrong. In this undertaking I always have to do everything myself.' He discovered that the main feed line had been snagged and severed, and even though he got the transformer working he could not make radio contact. 'Now the fault is supposed to be in the instrument itself! I am no radio mechanic and I can do no more to help. Tomorrow Pit must try with his instrument.'[23]

On 22 May they headed toward the Kharga Oasis. Almásy left another store of fuel and water to the south of Dakhla, in case he needed to take another route on the return journey. They then passed through an area where Almásy recalled hundreds of Sanusi refugees had been rescued by the Mamur of Dakhla, Abd er Rachman Zoher, who with two Fords had ferried them to the safety of the oasis. Forty would later die and a further 100 were not reached in time, but 300 had been saved. The Salam men saw the bleached white bones of humans and animals.

That evening Pit's (Sandstette's) transmitter was working but he could not raise Schildkroete at Jalo. What was Rommel's signals branch doing? Almásy was furious.

I have scarcely enough petrol to get back. Everything was discussed and planned in detail ... I was only to radio and they would drop fuel, water and food for me in any grid square I liked. Now the instrument which is tuned to our point of departure has fallen out and the called station on the other does not answer! Probably there's another shift going on there. I <u>begged</u> them to leave Schildkroete at one fixed point.[24]

Almásy had to reconsider his limited fuel supply; he might just reach his objective if he took the road to the Kharga Oasis instead of the fuel-consuming dunes. The road meant a greater chance of running into a British patrol, but he considered that he had no choice. Even if he reached Kharga safely he knew he still might not have enough fuel for the return journey, and would have to 'get petrol by cunning or force'.

That night they camped to the west of the Kharga Oasis. On 23 May they set off at the crack of dawn, prepared for a long day. Almásy was determined to get Pit and Pan as close to the Nile Valley city of Assiut as he could, but he wanted to be on his way back to Jalo before dark.

Nearing Kharga, Almásy told those in the following car to keep close, to stop when he stopped and to have their weapons at the ready. However, they were not to fire under any circumstances unless he did so first. They passed the railway station and on into the town square, where they were stopped by two *ghaffirs* (night watchmen-auxiliary police), one of whom was armed. Almásy coolly exchanged greetings in Arabic, and they told him to report to the *Markas*, the administration centre, where he would find their captain. Almásy countered by saying that he was merely carrying his Major's luggage to the railway station and was in a hurry to catch a train. One of the watchmen rode on Almásy's truck running board to point out the *Markas*, where they dropped him off.

In his account Eppler takes credit for getting them through the check point, claiming that he told the watchmen that he was an 'Egyptian Divisonal Interpreter attached to a British General', that the General was not far behind, was in a hurry and might 'tear a big strip off him' if delayed. According to him, at the mention of the General the *ghaffir* waved them on.[25]

They soon found the main road heading north and drove on through the oasis.

In the glow of the rising sun we drive through the most beautiful of all oases. On our right is the temple of Isis, then on the left the early Christian necropolis, the Roman citadel and the small watch towers and in between the most glorious spots of oasis with its bright green fields, the great shady *lebah* trees and the countless palms. The road is excellent.[26]

The road took them across the railway embankment, past the old POW camp at Moharig and along the Roman road which led on through the Yabsa Pass. At the Pass, Almásy stopped the party to have their photographs taken; in one shot he can be seen wearing his stained Afrika Korps uniform, standing beside a sign in English and Arabic: 'DANGEROUS DESCENT/DRIVE IN BOTTOM GEAR.'

At 14:00, having left one car and two men concealed not far behind, Almásy, Pit, Pan and Munz reached the edge of the Egyptian Plateau within sight of Assiut. According to Eppler, Almásy brought the vehicle to a halt and said, 'That's it, chaps. Let's keep it short.'

Eppler and Sandy – who would be known as Peter Monkaster from this point – changed into their civilian clothes.

I carefully checked all papers and other small details, such as my Egyptian driving licence, address book and club membership card – all those little things a man carries about with him in his pockets that prove he really is who he says he is … Almásy turned his truck around, the second truck followed him, and they were on their way back. [According to Almásy he did not take the second Ford to the drop-off point.] There we were, two agents who had to get to Cairo, despite the omnipresence of the British Army.[27]

Salam was over, *Kondor* had just begun.

17. Assiut

EPPLER AND SANDSTETTE SET OFF on their four-kilometre walk to Assiut, suitcases in hand. About two kilometres from the town they buried their German uniforms and a W/T set between two hills, marking the spot with a pile of stones.[1]

The original plan had called for Sandstette to stay in Assiut, while Eppler went on to Cairo. However the two men decided to stick together; when they decided this is not known. It may have been that Sandstette was uncomfortable travelling to or staying in the town alone. Eppler later observed that 'Sandy was no good at finding places.'[2]

The road the two men trudged along ran straight through a British Army camp. Sandy wondered whether this would spell the end of their mission, but Eppler told him to calm down. Their cover was good, for only a lunatic would attempt to get to Cairo by the route they had taken, no one would suspect them. They strode on.

They were stopped by the sentries and questioned by a Major. Eppler writes:

> I explained that our car was some way back behind the hill and that we had broken down. As we had managed to get this far, we should be grateful for a lift to the railway station, since we had to be in Cairo by the next day. I can still hear him asking in amazement. 'To the station? I can't do that without knowing who you are. We are not running a taxi service, you know.'[3]

The two men introduced themselves and showed the Major their passports. Eppler mentioned that his family were the 'Gaafars' and that the Englishman might have heard of them, his stepfather being a well known judge and pro-British. This broke the ice and they were invited to the officers' mess for a drink, while transport was arranged to take them to Assiut station. The 'cool whisky and soda' was wondrous after eleven days driving across the desert.

Some of the officers observed that they were fools to have gone into the desert without a second car. Eppler, who appears to have done most of the talking, agreed that they had been unwise. His account of events states that they were invited to stay for lunch, but this seems somewhat unlikely given the timing; according to Almásy the two agents were only dropped off in the desert at 14:00, so by the time they arrived at the British camp it would have been well past the lunch hour.[4]

Finally, after many thanks, they were driven to the station, no doubt relieved that their story had been swallowed. But they were well aware they might have to endure a rather more searching examination on the train or on arrival in Cairo. In their cases they were carrying thousands of pounds in sterling and Egyptian pounds, which no one in their right mind would be carrying. Furthermore, Sandy's case 'contained a very superior radio transmitter, purpose-built for long-distance communications work, a neat little 40-Watt transmitter/receiver.'[5] How would they talk themselves out of that?

Eppler reserved two first class seats on the late afternoon Luxor-Cairo express. He did not want their luggage placed in the baggage van and it was likely that the Field Security Police would be inspecting baggage on their arrival in Cairo.

While standing outside the booking office, still with their cases, they came across some Nubians also waiting for the train. These men explained that they hoped to obtain work in Cairo, and told Eppler that they were tribesmen from Dangola. He considered Nubians to be honest. 'Not even the missionaries, for all their painstaking efforts had succeeded in turning them into dishonest Africans.'

Eppler asked the youngest, who was about seventeen and called Mahmoud, if he would be interested in becoming his servant in Cairo. They haggled briefly over money, another essential convention, and then settled on £6 a month. For this princely sum Mahmoud assured him 'the prophet would this very day order you a divan from the heavenly carpenter, on which you should experience heavenly joys with three virgins, delivered fresh each day.' Eppler found the prospect pleasing, albeit he could not enjoy such a prospect until he departed 'from this wicked world'.[5]

Sandy was watching the luggage and was startled when Eppler returned with a servant who duly picked up their cases and walked off. He had been given enough money for a third-class ticket, and instructions to meet them at the exit of the Cairo main station.

Eppler assured Sandy, who was under the impression they would never see Mahmoud again, that no one would ever bother to check the Nubian. Arriving in Cairo that night they found their new servant waiting for them outside the station with their cases. They had trouble finding accommodation, but Eppler knew the city well and he was resourceful, finally finding them quarters in a brothel, the Pension Nadia, for two nights.

As Eppler and Sandy disappeared into the seedy districts of Cairo, British GHQ in the city still knew nothing of Operation *Salam* or *Kondor*. This was despite the best efforts of Jean Alington at Bletchley Park, and the work of Y Section of Eighth Army in the field (radio reconnaissance). A month was lost before the *Salam* intercepts were read and passed onto GHQ Cairo, and the British missed the opportunity to deploy the LRDG to intercept Almásy. A further problem was that the *Salam* commando had been unable to raise Schildkroete, so there was not much for the Allies to read once the agents set off. Bureaucracy at GHQ no doubt further delayed the flow of information due to the 'lassitude of the 'Long Range Shepherd's Group', the staff officers who spent most of their time propping up the bars in clubs and hotels like Shepheard's.[6]

It was not until 25 May that GHQ Cairo learned of Almásy's journey across the desert to Assiut. Even then LRDG might have been able to catch him on the return journey, but at that time all Kufra's patrols were out searching for three downed South African Air Force Blenheim bombers that had gone missing on a training flight three weeks earlier. It was only on 5 June that LRDG and SDF sent out patrols looking for Almásy. Captain Ken Lazorus' patrol found Almásy's fresh tracks at the Wadi el Aqaba, the main route through the Gilf Kebir. They mined the track and set up an observation post, but Almásy was long gone.[7]

18. The Flap

THREE DAYS AFTER EPPLER AND Sandy arrived in Cairo, Rommel launched his offensive, which he fully expected would bring his troops to the banks of the Nile. Auchinleck had originally intended to launch his own spring offensive in mid-May; however reports indicated that the Afrika Korps had received strong armoured reinforcements. The Allied Commander in Chief considered his strength to be inadequate and with the agreement of the War Cabinet in London the attack was postponed for a month, a fatal mistake, handing the initiative to Rommel.

Back in April Rommel had planned to attack on 26 May, which he duly did. His tactics for the Gazala battle were to pin the British armour down with a frontal assault in the north, 'where the Tommies had dug in … a technical marvel'.[1] The British defences consisted of a series of boxes, with powerful artillery and infantry dug in to resist even heavy air attacks. Between the boxes were extensive minefields. However the assault was a feint, and Rommel's main armoured thrust went south around the desert flank.

Auchinleck had instructed Ritchie not to deploy his armour to defend the boxes until he knew the intentions of the enemy, but this order was largely ignored. After three days the British armour had been severely mauled, and Rommel had planted his main force firmly behind the British position in an area that became known as the Cauldron. The battles here were bloody.

The British hoped to pin the German armour in the Cauldron, but one by one their defensive boxes were overrun. By mid-June Rommel was again at the gates of Tobruk. Both sides had suffered heavy casualties in the continuous fighting and Eighth Army's command structure began to collapse, leaving units fighting in isolation against hopeless odds. This earned them Rommel's admiration, as he praised the courage of the Allied soldiers.

General Ritchie felt he had no choice but to pull back. Auchinleck reluctantly agreed, but insisted that Tobruk be held at all costs. Defence of the port town was given to the South African Division and by 15

June Eighth Army had pulled back east of the city. The defences and minefields had been neglected since the successful defence in 1941, allowing the Germans to bring their guns much closer to the walls:

> Jerry had got a ring of their .88 millimetres right up now and were banging the shells onto the edge of the escarpment. The ricochets – perhaps they were doing it for that effect – were screaming out over the harbour in flat trajectory like a curtain of wailing rain. It was doing no damage, except to minds. But that was far the worst.[2]

On 20 June the Germans rolled over the defences of Tobruk after heavy air raids by the Luftwaffe. The attack came from an unexpected direction – the southeast. General H.B. Klopper had thought it would come from the southwest, and had promised to hold until 'the last man and the last round' but the town fell in a few hours. The German victors took 32,000 prisoners and a huge quantity of materiel, including 2000 trucks and large stores of fuel, food and ammunition.[3] It was 'a staggering blow to the British cause'.[4]

Rommel's order of the day for 21 June was as follows:

> Soldiers of the Panzer Army Afrika! Now we must utterly destroy the enemy. During the coming days I shall be making great demands upon you once more so that we may reach our goal.[5]

His officers could almost taste the whiskys and soda waiting for them at Shepheard's Hotel. Rommel was promoted to Field Marshal by Hitler and the Italian Generals Cavallero and Bastico were also promoted to Field Marshals by Mussolini.

The fall of Tobruk heralded the 'Flap' in Egypt; it was not the first in the war, but probably the most serious. Hermione Ranfurly wrote of it in her diary: '22 June. The Germans have taken Tobruk. No news has shocked us more since Dunkirk.'[6]

At the end of June, with Alexandria the first likely target for the Afrika Korps, Admiral Henry Harwood – who had commanded the British squadron at the Battle of the River Plate, and had taken over command of the Mediterranean Fleet from Admiral Cunningham in April – had little choice but to disperse his fleet to other ports. Units were moved to Port Said, Haifa and Beirut without warning;

suddenly people found the harbour empty and fear mounted in the city. British government offices began burning their files and British women and children packed up their homes and joined crowds at the station. Others set off across the Delta in cars crammed with possessions. With the loss of the protection of the Royal Navy the European community felt abandoned. The BBC did not help by calling the battle around El Alamein the 'Battle for Egypt'.[7] Meanwhile Egyptian shops and clubs in the city began displaying decorations welcoming the German troops.

On 29 June Alexandria suffered several heavy air raids and the 'Flap' quickly spread across the Delta to Cairo. Alfred Sansom was swept up in it:

> British wives and children were evacuated to Palestine and to the Sudan, so swiftly that when I phoned my wife to tell her to pack she had already gone. I was told that if Cairo fell I was to stay behind with a few picked men to carry out specified acts of sabotage, after which we were to lie low until our troops recaptured the city.[8]

1 July became famous in the city as 'Ash Wednesday', the day when the British Embassy and GHQ started burning mountains of files. Sansom was engaged in this job:

> Meanwhile secret documents were already being burnt. Large incinerators had been placed on the roof of Red Pillars, as the headquarters in Kasr el Aini was called, and I was responsible for the safe transfer of documents scheduled for destruction. This operation was hardly over when one of my NCOs brought some peanuts from a street-vendor and found they were wrapped up in a paper marked 'Most Secret'.[9]

It turned out that a strong wind had blown many highly classified papers out of the open incinerators before they were burnt, and scattered them over the city. Afterwards Lieutenant-General T.W. Corbett, Chief of Staff to Auchinleck, was condemned for his handling of the 'Flap'.

To make matters worse there was a run on the banks. The Note Issue rose from £57 million on 25 June, to £76 million on 4 July, and note production had to be started in Egypt as supplies from England could not keep pace with demand. The Egyptian government considered moving itself and the gold reserves to Khartoum.

Soon after Eppler arrived in Cairo (in early June) he had observed that 'If it had not been for the presence of so many British soldiers, you would never have thought that a few hundred kilometres to the west a dreadful war was raging in Libya.'[10] By 10 June 'Cairo was in turmoil … foreign currency on the black market dropped 50 per cent and the true value of British money could only be had from the paymaster corps.' Amongst the thousands of 'Jews, Greeks, and the flotsam of various nationalities – that is, amongst those who had enough money – the cry went up: "Let's get out!"'[11]

As in Alexandria, the native Cairo civilian population viewed the likely arrival of the Germans with mixed feelings. Many, although they hated the British, felt they were on to a good thing business-wise and doubted that the Germans would be such a soft touch. Shares slumped on the stock exchange while property prices dropped to pre-war levels. Strangely enough, many Jews elected to stay in Cairo rather than go to Palestine – where sooner or later they thought there would be trouble with the local militant Jews – and furthermore the Palestine administration was slow in issuing visas. However, news of the German treatment of Jews had travelled as far as Cairo, and many others sold their properties and businesses at a loss before fleeing.

Sansom and the Field Security Service were at full stretch, carrying out a series of arrests of people sympathetic to the Germans. The information they obtained was generally trivial, such as the list compiled by the Endozzi Sisters – who had worked at the Italian Legation – which detailed members of the Italian community who were sympathetic to the British, and which they intended to hand over to the Axis forces when they arrived. Relatives betrayed relatives for all sorts of ulterior motives. 'Another faithless wife offered to let me sleep with her every Friday if I would lock up her Italian husband, who happened to be a loyal member of the anti-Fascist group that helped us to compile the lists.'[12] These more harmless suspects were housed at the Italian school at Boulac.

It was a rough business for Sansom, who was beaten up twice in a short period of time. On the first occasion he was attacked by an Italian fascist who had escaped internment from Boulac; Sansom caught up with him in a bar and 'all hell broke loose.' He suffered a black eye after being hit with a beer bottle, but he got his man. The second occasion was more serious. He came across a group of drunken New Zealanders who were beating up a gharry driver, and when he went to the man's assistance he got the worst of it. Fortunately he was rescued by two policemen but ended up in hospital with two broken ribs, 'and my face looked as if I had just made an unsuccessful challenge for the World's Heavyweight Championship.'[13]

A more important aspect of Sansom's work was keeping the militant nationalist Egyptians under observation, in particular the Free Officers movement within the army. Anwar el Sadat was one of the movement's members, then a Lieutenant in the signals branch. He and a group of likeminded officers had penned a treaty ready to place before Rommel, stating that the German commander could count on them and their resistance movement. He was in contact with the Axis forces, a fact he rather foolishly confided to his diary, which was found along with an English translation of *Mein Kampf* in which some paragraphs were underlined in red ink, when he was later arrested.[14]

Sansom had put one of his best men, Sergeant Wilson, on the job to watch El Sadat. 'Without knowing it I had started on what was to be my biggest spy-catching operation of the war.'While undercover, Wilson was approached by an attractive Arab girl called Zahira Ezzet, the sister of a Copt that Sansom had advised might be a good contact to cultivate within the Sadat group. She told him she wanted a plan of GHQ, saying rather lamely that she just wanted to see it. Wilson reported this to Sansom, who encouraged him to cultivate the relationship.

Zahira's brother, Lieutenant Hassan Ezzet, was soon convinced that Wilson knew GHQ like the back of his hand. Sansom was surprised at this; surely they already knew the place well?

GHQ had always been my main security headache. So many people, including a lot of civilians, were going in and out all day that I was always afraid of a leakage at the top. The very fact of working at GHQ made people careless, and officers would exchange information over the internal telephone, for example, without a thought about the girls on the exchange. As far as possible these were ATS girls from Britain, but quite a few were locally enlisted. And then there were all the civilian employees. Of course they had been carefully vetted, but no security screening system in the world is fool proof …[15]

Sansom told Wilson not to give into the girl too easily or it might arouse suspicion. Wilson played hard to get but finally agreed to supply a plan to her brother for £100, although naturally it would be completely fabricated.

Sansom had a trap laid to pick up Ezzet at the handover in a cafe. However the Lieutenant slipped the net, as he found a 'big Chevrolet car waiting for him with three men inside'. The British gave chase through the streets and alleys of the city, which only ended when Ezzet and his companions finally abandoned their car and fled into a house.

> Some shots were fired, I received a glancing blow from a chair on the side of my head as we forced an entry, but no serious damage was done. We arrested the four men with the worthless plan which Ezzet had carefully preserved throughout the chase. With this evidence against him we were able to get him a sentence of five years hard labour.

However, something struck Sansom as odd about the whole affair: what did Ezzet want a plan of GHQ for? He concluded it must mean

> … a German paid spy was planning to penetrate the building and steal information, and he wanted to know the location of the offices most likely to provide it. I could not see the Copt playing the role himself.[16]

Field Security had been alerted to the possibility of a German spy within the city.

19. Kondor Calling

AFTER LEAVING THE BROTHEL, PENSION Nadia, Eppler and Sandy looked for a more permanent base. They took a flat belonging to Madame Therese Guillemet, a Frenchwoman married to an Egyptian, at No 8 Sharia Boursa el Guedida. They rented the rooms for three months, paying £75 rent in advance; Sandy kept a record of the money they spent.[1]

It soon proved unsuitable, as when Sandy set up an aerial on the roof and sent out his call sign he got no reply. He concluded that he was sending a poor signal owing to the flat being surrounded by taller buildings. There was also the problem that the flat had once been the haunt of prostitutes, and former clients and the police were frequently at the door. Therese, the owner, lived with them, and she herself had once been a prostitute and a madam. One day her pimp, Albert Wahda, visited and recognised Eppler, whom he knew as Hussein Gaafar. Eppler explained away his absence from Cairo since 1937 by saying that he had been living at a farm at Assiut.[2]

Following this encounter Eppler immediately began looking for more suitable accommodation through people he met in night-clubs, cabarets and bars. He also hoped these contacts would lead to information that might interest Rommel. It also became crucial for the agents to change their British currency, which they found was not in use in Egypt, and those using it were at risk of being arrested. They had little choice but to change it on the black market for a third or half its value. But there were plenty of takers, few of whom were entirely trustworthy.

Eppler visited his mother in old Cairo at 10 Sharia Masr al Kasa; while there he learnt that his stepfather had died several months before. His stepbrother Hassan Gaafar was not at home and he told his mother not to tell him of his visit.[3]

The two agents continued to make the rounds of the Cairo night-clubs, making sure to spend heavily – an average of £20 a night – and gaining many acquaintances, most of whom were worthless.[4] On the roof garden of the Continental Hotel Eppler asked Rossier, the head waiter, to introduce them to the celebrated belly dancer Hekmat Fahmy.[5] Eppler's account states that he had known her 'for some considerable time – and not only in my official capacity. I wanted her to work for me.' He found the roof garden intoxicating:

> The sweet scent of a thousand roses in bloom mingled with the French perfumes of brown- and white-skinned women. The figures round the tables were barely discernible in the subdued light that filtered through the flowering shrubs in which lamps were concealed. Stinking rich Egyptians, Greeks, and Armenians, who could not have cared less about the awful war, were making up to assorted lovelies hung with precious jewels.

According to Eppler, he actually met Sansom at the Continental Hotel bar. The Englishman was drinking 'White Horse and soda' and proceeded to introduce himself as 'Sansom' which seems highly unlikely, given the latter's careful nature. Eppler also states that Sansom 'could hold his liquor. In the end I left owing him a round.' Eppler also left with Hekmat.[6]

Sansom himself says that he first saw Eppler much later at the Kit Kat Cabaret (see Chapter 21) lighting a cigarette with a £5 note, saying: 'There are plenty more where that came from.' Sansom also states that he gave Eppler a fictitious Egyptian name.[7]

After the agents had a second meeting with Hekmat Fahmy at the Continental she agreed to put them up for a night on her *dahabia* (houseboat) at Agouza on the Nile. Eppler suggests the night he spent with Hekmat was not merely business.

> I discussed everything with Hekmat during the remainder of the night, in her fabulously furnished houseboat, while we lay in her wide sensuous bed under its silken mosquito net. [We perfected our] plans down to the last detail.[8]

This again is unlikely given Sandy's presence; did he play gooseberry? During interrogation after their capture, both men denied sleeping with Hekmat and stated that Albert Wahda was on the boat that night as well.[9] The pimp seems to have latched onto them no doubt for easy money, but he was useful as a messenger and gofer.

However, there is no doubt that Eppler was infatuated with the belly dancer, an infatuation that may have gone back several years:

> She was extremely beautiful, and justifiably the most adored of belly dancers. She had a head of lustrous black hair, and sensational green eyes inherited from a Circassian grandmother. Her nose was the delicate aristocratic nose found in ancient Egyptian paintings of women. As she sat there, she had that same dreamy face to be seen on the bas-reliefs of God knows how many dynasties in upper Egypt. Her features were so finely drawn they were almost stylized, but wonderfully lively. Her skin had a tawny colour that was the perfect foil for her deep green eyes.[10]

It seems the reality was that during that night on the houseboat the two men slept in the room of Hekmat's lover, a British officer who was away in the desert. They proceeded to go through his personal gear, and thought they had hit the jackpot when they found a map of the defences of Tobruk, until they realised that it was an Italian map dating from before the British occupation.

Hekmat herself denied having anything to do with Eppler and Sandy's espionage activities, or even showing them her lover's papers. No doubt she was willing to pass on any pillow talk gleaned from British officers, much as her colleagues on the belly dancing circuit did for a financial consideration, but she was no Mata Hari.[11]

However Hekmat did help the agents find another *dahabia* to live in at Agouza, near the Egyptian Benevolent Hospital. It appeared an ideal solution to their problems, and they agreed to pay £12 a month for the boat with a £30 deposit.[12] Eppler described it as 'a very attractive dahabia, with a great sundeck complete with a bar of mahogany'. The bar was well stocked, and he was glad to see that below decks it was well furnished to a near exotic degree, with soft divans and gossamer curtains. It had two ladders leading below decks, which he felt was good as 'one might need them in a hurry.' Sandy found a good hiding place for his transmitter under a radiogram, and the aerials on deck were unlikely to attract attention.[13]

According to Eppler, only the first transmission Sandy made from the houseboat was acknowledged by the German receiving station in the desert. It is unlikely that even this attempt was successful, as by this time *Kondor* had been abandoned by Rommel (see below). Further attempts, usually made at midnight, also proved fruitless.[14] They began to wonder if their transmitter set was faulty. It did not occur to them that something could be wrong the other end, and that the Abwehr had neglected to give them an alternative contact in case of a change in operations.

***

Meanwhile Almásy's return trip across the desert had not gone entirely smoothly. After leaving Eppler and Sandstette, he set off back on his 1400-mile journey; picking up the waiting second car 'we waste no time.' They reached Yabsa Pass in darkness; 'After a quick decision I have the camouflage paint removed from the searchlights (headlights) and we drive down the steep snaking road with all lights on.' They covered 420 kilometres that day (260 miles).

The next day the two cars passed through Kharga once again. In the town square they saw one of the *ghaffirs* they had seen the day before, but he did not stop them. Perhaps he did not recognise them straight away, but clearly he soon figured it out as Almásy saw him running after them in the rear view mirror.

At the railway station they stopped to take photographs of cereal supplies, and learnt from the locals that there was not much traffic about. On the strength of this information Almásy decided to stay on the road. 'I can spare myself a good bit of miserable terrain if I just drive along the Kharga-Dachla road and turn off just before Dachla to the south, to disappear into the great void.'[15]

He was concerned that he would not find the tracks they had made on the outward journey, but in fact he did, although it was difficult owing to a covering of drifting sand. Occasionally the tracks disappeared altogether and the men had to get out of their vehicles and search on foot. This was time consuming but saved precious fuel. Fortunately, Almásy found one of their fuel dumps shortly after they lost the tracks altogether. He also found a large snake who had set up home amidst the drums, which viewed them with 'glowing emerald eyes. Munz want to kill it, but I tell him that it is the *djinn* of our hiding place and hence of our return journey too, which visibly impresses the men.'[16]

They picked up 'Flitzer' – the abandoned Bedford – and still managed to cover 250 miles that day. On 25 May they set off late at 09.30, as Almásy had given them 'a bit of a rest'. The three vehicles headed due west toward the Gilf Kebir, Almásy's navigation was 'perfectly correct', picking up his 1933 track. They found their fuel dump at the 'Two Breasts' – managing to do so without getting any of the vehicles stuck – and camped in the 'Great Breck'.

On 26 May Almásy stumbled across enemy vehicles in several columns near the Drei Burgen (Three Castles). Crossing the skyline of a ridge, he saw that 'parked trucks of an enemy column of 28 vehicles were camping.' The *Salam* commandos quickly got off the ridge and hid in dead ground, then Almásy returned to the crest on foot. He saw another enemy column about three miles east of the first, and another farther out on the plain. However, he concluded that none had seen his party.

Almásy needed to get through the Wadi Anag

> … to get out of the mountains via the Bab-el-Masr Pass before these columns. In a state of 'alert' with the MG ready to open up, I drove by compass, toward the Wadi Anag. Before we enter the protection of the gorge the first vehicles of a column appear barely 4 km behind us, on the skyline. Had they seen us?[17]

Having found their second Bedford and fuel dump, it was obvious that they could not go on with four vehicles and four men, as there would be no one to man the machine gun. They need to refuel and change tyres, and while his men worked, Almásy watched the enemy. He soon realised that they must be from the Sudan Defence Force, as they stopped for prayers at midday, giving the Commando some respite. But he knew he would not be able to shake them off on the narrow mountain track: 'Between here and Bab-el-Masr there is no chance of evasion.' Subterfuge was the only answer; he let one column pass and then joined the track, with another enemy column not far behind.

> I do not think that the guard on the six vehicles behind has seen our three vehicles. After a few minutes we are driving along the tracks of the column itself. I had the MG inside the vehicle so that it should not

> give us away. We went quietly KM after KM and I could already see
> the large circular sole of the valley on the far side of which is situated
> the narrow entrance of Bab-el-Masr. The enemy column is bivouacked
> just in front of the entrance.[18]

As they passed the enemy camp – keeping the sun in the eyes of the
SDF column – they saluted, which was returned, the markings of
their vehicles too dull to be seen clearly. They had got away with it,
and drove through the tight entrance to the Bab-el-Masr. Seven miles
on, the left back tyre of Almásy's car got a puncture. 'Good job that
did not happen near the enemy column,' observed Almásy.[19]

By 27 May the group had reached the Hauwaisch Mountains
along the 'blessed smugglers' road', and arrived at 'No1 camp with
petrol store'. The run that day was 340km (210 miles).[20]

On 29 May they had a leisurely morning, shaving and washing.
In order to get to Jalo they had to drain the fuel from the 'President'
into the 'Inspector', but they intended to return for the vehicle. Only
'Flitzer' – left at the Gilf Kebir – was truly abandoned.

> Exactly at noon we came to the first kilometre on the southern edge
> of the Gialo [Jalo] aerodrome. Whilst Munz fired the pre-arranged 3
> white flares we hoisted the tricolour [Italian flag] on the aerial mast of
> the car under the aegis of which we had started our trip and had suc-
> cessfully terminated it.[21]

It was certainly an outstanding achievement for Almásy and his men,
who had operated in the LRDG's back yard unnoticed. Almásy
soon retrieved his vehicles from the desert south near Jalo, and
then travelled to Tripoli where they were handed over to the Wido
Commando for operations against the Free French in the Tibesti.

Almásy was at the German Consulate on 2 June where the
Abwehr were keen to contact him; the station chief Holzbrecher was
instructed to make sure that *Kondor* had good contact, and to send
Salam (Almásy) to Afrika Korps HQ communications 'in order to
start traffic with Condor working'.[22]

Almásy duly rushed to report to Rommel who by then was direct-
ing the assault on the Free French position at Bar Hacheimn toward
the southern end of Eighth Army's Gazala Line.

'Herr General, Operation *Salam* successfully concluded. Operation *Kondor* can now begin,' he reported to the C-in-C.[23]

Rommel appeared awkward. In May he had brought Aberle and Weber from Mamelin, where they seemed underemployed, to join his HQ signals staff, which was short of operators. He had argued that they could wait for messages with his staff just as well as elsewhere and lend a hand. But the heavy fighting of 27 and 28 May meant that the Afrika Korps was in danger behind the Gazala Line. Even Rommel had to flee one morning half shaved when his HQ came under attack from the LRDG.

In the confusion the truck with Aberle and Weber and all the *Kondor* material was captured. The operation was compromised and had to be abandoned. It was ordered that all messages from the agents in Cairo were to be ignored from then on.[24]

Almásy was stunned. The Abwehr had gone to so much trouble to help Rommel and he had thrown it away, for the sake of two radio operators being idle for a few days. *Kondor* was dead before it had truly begun.

Rommel congratulated Almásy on his efforts and promoted him to Major on the spot. Later he was awarded the Iron Cross First and Second Class. He told the disappointed Hungarian not to worry, for he hoped to arrive on the Nile 'with my whole army by a shorter route' than *Salam* had taken. Almásy answered acidly that a villa would be prepared for Rommel on the Nile, 'provided the British haven't captured you in the meantime.'[25] A few weeks later Almásy was on his way home, suffering from acute amoebic dysentery picked up on Operation *Salam*.

20. The Ring Tightens

WHEN ROMMEL BARELY ESCAPED THE clutches of New Zealanders of the LRDG, a bullet is said to have ripped one of the epaulettes off his uniform jacket as he sped off in his car with his driver. Aberle and Weber, along with others from the Abwehr signals unit, were not so lucky and were captured. The captives were briefly questioned at Eighth Army HQ before being hurried on to Cairo for a more thorough interrogation by intelligence officers. Thus the *Rebecca Code* had been compromised before Eppler and Sandstette had even arrived in the city.[1]

Aberle and Weber were taken to the interrogation centre at Maadi near Cairo. At first all they would say were their names and numbers and throughout the process they remained pretty tight lipped. However, one of the men brought in to look them over did not need them to speak. This mysterious man from the Defence Security Office was called 'Robby' by Leonard Mosley, who interviewed him,[2] and 'Bob' by Sansom in his account. He was undoubtedly an MI6 operative.[3] He worked for Cuthbert Bowly, head of MI6 in Cairo at the time, who had responsibility for the Balkans and the Middle East. He established good working relations with GHQ and other security services, but was overworked and his health suffered, resulting in a short spell in hospital toward the end of 1941. The Rebecca Code must surely have crossed his desk at this time.[4]

'Robby'/'Bob' looked over Aberle and Weber's possessions and came across a copy of *Rebecca*. It was the only book they had with them; other reading matter consisted of Nazi magazines and newspapers and personal letters from home. An interview with them confirmed that their knowledge of English literature was about nil, and their English was poor, so why did they have an English language copy of the novel?

A forensic photographer from GHQ soon worked out from the yellow dust jacket that the book had been priced at 50 escudos (the Germans had tried to remove the price) and had therefore been bought in Portugal. The MI6 man's report to GHQ stated that in his opinion a significant German agent had started operations in the area.

He is probably a German national with close knowledge of Egypt and the Egyptians. He is regarded by his bosses as an operator of such importance that they have provided him with his own personal code and a special listening-unit to take the information he collects. We have fortunately collected the listening-unit in the persons of Aberle and Weber.[5]

Reports passed through the Defence Security Office in Cairo, across the desk of Colonel G.J. Jenkins, and on to the War Office and MI5 in London.[6]

About the same time the radio monitoring section at GHQ reported a transmitter coming on air precisely at midnight, almost certainly somewhere in the city, using a code. It was always the same, a sending station's identification which was not acknowledged. Sansom had received reports on this, which remained a puzzle until a man called 'Bob' showed him the copy of *Rebecca* he had taken from Aberle and Weber's kit. Sansom admitted to having read the novel when it was first published and Bob's information revealed the truth behind the transmissions.

Things began to click into place. The Germans were using *Rebecca* as a code manual. Their agent in Cairo was transmitting in code. He was not yet sending information because he was not getting acknowledgment; and knowing that he was probably being monitored, he was not going to help us to locate his transmitter by broadcasting uselessly. [With Aberle and Weber in captivity] the only place receiving the spy was our own monitoring unit in Cairo. But this state of affairs was not going to last long. The Germans were bound to answer from another station before long. Then our chaps would jam the pirate, the Germans would tell him he was being jammed, and he would do a bunk.[7]

The spies themselves were already beginning to wonder what was going on. Was there something wrong with their W/T set? Sandstette and Eppler had no other means to contact their controllers.

Eppler wrote to his stepbrother, Hassan Gaafar, who was back in Cairo and asked to meet him at the 'American Bar'. There Eppler – disguised in dark glasses – picked up his brother and took him back to the houseboat, where Hassan met Sandy. Together they explained their predicament: their transmitter needed repairs, perhaps a new quartz. Hassan agreed to help them.[8]

Hassan contacted Viktor Hauer, a German working at the Swedish Legation, who looked after the interests of Germans in Egypt. Hassan took Hauer to the houseboat on 12 July, bringing with them an American W/T set which had been stored at the Legation. Hauer also brought a Mauser pistol with ammunition and some maps of Egypt.[9]

Apart from the problems of communication, the agents were also having difficulties making useful local contacts. Their main contact was supposed to have been Mohamed Mamza, whom Eppler had known before the war, but they soon learned that he had been taken into detention. However, the Hungarian priest Pere Demetriou, based at the Church of St Theresa Shoubra, had a spare Abwehr W/T set left over from the failed Operation *El Masri* (see Chapter 7). Almásy had advised Eppler to contact Brother Demetriou on his arrival; he was sure the priest 'would give them all assistance'. Maybe they could even work with their own set from the church.[10]

In his account Eppler says he did contact Demetriou, travelling to the chapel of St Mark's school on the Shariah Ibn el-Kourang in Hekmat's borrowed Cadillac.

> I was supposed to talk to a priest who would be celebrating early morning Mass. Should I be unlucky, I would have to keep coming to the church until I had found the right man.

He knew there was another W/T set somewhere in the city but,

> I hated this kind of set-up; it could so easily turn out to be a trap. I disliked contacts that had been arranged by other people ...[11]

Entering the church he found several parishioners taking mass; he had to wait uneasily in one of the pews until the service was over. Finally, after exchanging code words in a secluded corner, he met the priest; he was more elderly than he had expected, his skin like leather after years in the sun. He had a 'lean face with a shock of white hair crowning it, the dark eyes' had a 'humorous twinkle'.

They retreated to the 'semi-darkness' of the vestry. Eppler asked him why no signals had been sent by him 'for some time'. Demetriou explained that since the failure of Operation *El Masri*, the British had captured many of those involved. The risks were too great. Eppler felt he would get little help from the priest.

> I knew that I would never return, not only because things were so dicey, but also because I could not approve of installing a transmitter under the altar of a church and, moreover operating it from there. That was asking for more brass neck than I had.

Obviously Demetriou had no such qualms on that score.[12]

The priest had had close contacts with the Hungarian Legation, which was no doubt where he came across Almásy; eventually it closed down its interests and switched to the Swedish Legation. There Demetriou met Hauer but it seems the latter did not quite trust the priest, and this may have rubbed off on Eppler.[13]

By this time Eppler was concerned that they were running out of money and had achieved little. He decided he must somehow get back to the Afrika Korps to find out what was happening. To this end he once again turned to Hauer who put him in touch with Fatma Amer, the Viennese wife of an Egyptian official who lived at Sharia Miquas 50 on Roda Island. Eppler observed that the Austrian woman 'had been assimilated so well by her surroundings that she would have passed unobserved as an Egyptian.'[14] However, Eppler was far from pleased with her or Hauer, complaining that they had no idea what they were doing and Hauer had 'brought him a transmitting set which was as inefficient as his own.'[15]

Fatma Amer was described by DSO Colonel Jenkins as 'a most dangerous woman, a brilliant actress, and a convincing liar'.[16] She worked on the fringes of the Abwehr, helped Axis escapees and had contacts with the pro-Nazi Egyptian group the Liberty Party. On 21 July she introduced Eppler to Abdel Moneim Salama who took him to meet an Egyptian Air Force officer at a coffee house in Gizeh, near the Abbas Bridge. It was Lieutenant Hassan Ezzet (see Chapter 18).

Eppler was far from happy talking there but Ezzet assured him that he was amongst friends. Eppler relented, and in a lowered voice he explained Sandy's and his predicament. What he needed was to be flown back to the Afrika Korps, and surely an Egyptian Air Force officer was in the position to do so. Ezzet said he was willing to meet

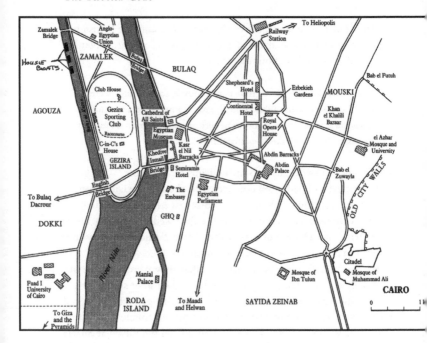

The centre of Cairo, 1939–1945.

Eppler again once he had checked the agents out; after all, he needed assurances that they were who they said they were if he was going to fly them back to Rommel, probably from near the pyramids of Giza. He suggested they meet on 23 July with Aziz el Masri Pasha; Eppler had little choice and agreed, well aware of the lack of success surrounding El Masri.

Hassan Ezzet dropped Eppler back at Fatma Amer's house. There to his surprise he met El Masri himself. The General sat in a chair too high for his diminutive frame, his feet not touching the ground, quite at ease smoking a cigarette in a jewelled holder. The two men talked long into the night about Eppler's need to return to the Afrika Korps and about El Masri's hopes for Egypt's great Aryan future. Eppler thought he had an overblown opinion of himself.[17]

The next night Eppler and his stepbrother Hassan Gaafar went by taxi to meet Ezzet at the Kubeh Garden Station at 21:00. They met by the ice box, where Ezzet told them 'We cannot talk here. I am being watched.' He told them to wait at the petrol station 500 yards away near the Egyptian Army Hospital on Sharia Ismail Bey. At the station they paid off the taxi and waited at bus stop No 10 on the main Cairo-Heliopolis road for half an hour, when a brown car finally pulled up, driven by El Masri. With him was Ezzet and Captain Anwar el Sadat, a captain of signals in the Egyptian Army. Eppler sent his stepbrother home and got into the General's car. They took the Heliopolis road and then drew up near the Villa Baron Empain to talk.[18]

Ezzet was still not happy, and wanted more proof that Eppler was whom he claimed to be. Eppler was frustrated and well aware of the risks involved, but said that all he could do was take them to his boat and introduce them to Sandstette. Ezzet tried to reassure him that the guarantee of his 'bona fides' was vital because he had no news from 'his man' Seoudi, who had flown over the German lines about two weeks before. Seoudi had been given letters of introduction from Masri Pasha and also code lists, as apparently he was supposed to establish a W/T link with him. He had also taken with him 1500 aerial photos of military installations and objectives in Egypt. Anwar el Sadat boasted that one of the targets they had photographed had already been bombed by the GAF (Luftwaffe). 'From this conversation it was quite clear to Eppler that Mazri [Masri] Pasha gave orders to Hassan and Hassan to Seoudi.'[19]

Fatma Amer had already told Eppler that Seoudi had been the pilot of one of two planes 'flown over to the Germans. One of them was shot down, the other arrived.' It appears Seoudi did fly over the German lines with the photographs; he gave a signal of friendship, but as he was flying a British Gladiator he was shot down.[20]

El Masri drove them back to the petrol station, then Eppler, Hassan Ezzet and Anwar el Sadat took a taxi to the Kit Kat Cabaret where they picked up Sandstette and drove on to the houseboat. There Ezzet told Eppler and Sandstette that he was in contact with the Germans through an agent in the town of Zagazig, in the Nile Delta, and that he could contact the Abwehr for them. Sandy wrote a message to Angelo, their operator, Major Seubent, of 1 H West, Abwehr:

Please guarantee our existence. We are in mortal danger. Please use the wave-length No 1 at 09:00hrs Tripoli time. Max and Moritz [their code names].[21]

Ezzet told them that it would take about six days to get a reply.

Anwar el Sadat examined the W/T sets that Sandy had been planning to ditch in the Nile, but changed his mind when the Captain told him that they were in working order. El Sadat was shocked by the obviously riotous life Eppler and Sandy were enjoying. There were empty bottles lying everywhere and evidence of female company. He wrote that the houseboat was

> … a place straight out of the *Thousand and One Nights,* where everything invited indolence, voluptuousness and pleasure of the senses. In this dissolute atmosphere the young Nazis had forgotten the delicate mission with which they had been entrusted.[22]

Eppler was equally unimpressed with El Masri and El Sadat, and felt that the meetings with them 'proved a waste of time'. They needed El Sadat's expert opinion on the radios, but the man went off in a huff making it clear that

> He did not approve of the cover we had chosen, although it was none of his business. He took it for granted that an agent ought to live like a hermit.

But Eppler had other worries and did not care how things looked to the Egyptian.

> I was fed up … I felt like a blind man having to grope without knowing where he is. I felt as browned off as a man on whom an enormous invisible fist descends every second, beating him into the ground. It was all very depressing.

But he cheered himself up with an 'outsize Scotch, four fingers of it, without soda …'[23]

Eppler doubtless would have been more depressed if he had known his file as Hussein Gaafar had already crossed Major Sansom's desk, along with those of El Masri, Anwar el Sadat, Hassan Ezzet and many others.

21. Currency Matters

THERE IS NO DOUBT THAT Eppler and Sandstette were undone by their actions. Colonel Jenkins in his report of August 1942 highlighted this.

> They were too intoxicated with the possession of so much money and too intent upon enjoying the 'fleshpots' of Egypt in the form of women and wine.[1]

This appears to have been true; why did Eppler act in such a risky manner? He must have known that it was dangerous to draw attention to themselves.

Long before he met Eppler, Sansom became aware of a Rifle Brigade Lieutenant buying people drinks in large quantities and paying in Sterling. The first report came from the Turf Club, a favourite haunt of British officers, an all-male establishment at 32 Sharia Adly Pasha.

> [It] would not have looked out of place in St James's street. A few minutes' walk from there brought one to Shepheard's Hotel, which after the Pyramids, was the most famous tourist landmark in Cairo.[2]

By the time Sansom got to the club the bird had flown. But he took away the money spent by the mysterious Rifle Brigade officer who had

> ... spent a few English pound notes and one fiver. There was nothing illegal in this, it just struck me as 'odd', for the forces were all paid in Egyptian currency. Apart from a few notes, probably sent by relatives in letters, English money was hardly ever seen.[3]

Using the barman's description of the mysterious man, Sansom checked out the Rifle Brigade officers who could have been in Cairo at the time. He came up blank; however, while there were many reasons for someone masquerading as an officer, Sansom knew that spending that amount of money pointed toward shady dealings, perhaps espionage. But surely the Abwehr knew that the British forces were usually paid in Egyptian currency?

> The only plausible explanation of the affair seemed to me that the Germans had made a colossal blunder of the most elementary kind. They had provided one of their agents with the wrong currency for the country in which he was operating.[4]

The Rifle Brigade officer was in fact Eppler, who by this time had only Sterling to spend. Several different people had been changing money for the two spies on the black market, although Albert Wahba, the pimp, seemed to be the main money changer. He boasted on one occasion that he was carrying '£15,000 in my pocket. I have to do all their business. They cannot do without me.'[5]

Eventually Eppler and Sandy were forced to spend British currency openly, as ultimately even the black market would not accept Sterling at any price.

Sansom had also found out the rate of exchange on the black market, and that, as one of his NCOs reported, 'None of the usual operators will touch Sterling. They must think Rommel has got us licked.'[6] The money business was both a help and a hindrance to Sansom and his men.

> I told the men to watch out for English money spenders in bars and cabarets … I warned them not to do anything that might put our quarry on his guard, and inevitably this hamstrung them somewhat. They could not go round asking direct questions about the currency-spending for fear that he would hear of it and be scared off. That was one reason why my men failed to get any lead. Another reason was that, as I had feared from the beginning the man we were after had realized he was suspected at the Turf Club.
>
> I learnt afterwards that was the last occasion Hans Eppler wore British Army uniform in Cairo. So in looking for a Rifle Brigade subaltern we were chasing a phantom – although, of course, we were not counting on the spy always to wear the same kind of clothes.[7]

According to Eppler it was after the meeting with Anwar El Sadat and Hassan Ezzet on the houseboat that he learnt that some of the currency he had been supplied and had changed was counterfeit. He had just poured his four fingers of Scotch and was sitting on one of the deck bar stools when 'Sami, the money-changer came up the gangway.' After Eppler poured him a gin, Sami told him that his pounds were counterfeit.

'Nonsense! What are you talking about?' Eppler was stunned by more bad news.

After a lengthy discussion Sami said that he was still willing to get rid of Eppler's remaining Sterling but that it would be 'expensive'. On the black market they would have to know they were 'duds'. 'An hour later, we were with a really dirty crook. He took them for a quarter of their face value, but at least I was rid of them.'

The next day Eppler told Sandy what had happened; the latter's reaction was pithy to say the least. 'No radio contact, up to our arses in hot notes – if you ask me, some bastard is trying to set us up.'[8]

Meanwhile Sansom had the money left by Eppler at the Turf Club flown to England to be checked out by experts at the Bank of England. They traced the pound notes to deposits in neutral countries including Switzerland and Spain; the five pound note was a forgery, certainly a product of the German government.

The British security services were already aware that Germany was forging currency. Operation *Bernhard* was the codename given to the German plan to destabilise the British economy by flooding the country with forged sterling notes in £5, £10, £20 and £50 denominations. The plan was named after SS Major Bernard Kruger, who set up a team of counterfeiters from inmates at Sachsenhausen concentration camp, beginning in 1942. By the end of the war they had produced 8,965,080 banknotes including US dollars, with a face value of £134,610,810. The notes are believed to be amongst the best counterfeits ever produced.[9]

The scheme to destabilise the British economy was never put into effect; rather the currency were used to pay for strategic imports and to fund German secret agents operating abroad. One of the most famous and successful German spies, 'Cicero' Elyesa Bazna, a Turk of Albanian origins, was paid with counterfeit notes. L.C. Mayzisch wrote an account of his service as Bazna's operator:

> He had received from me notes to the value of £300,000, or rather over a million dollars at the then rate of exchange, in bundles of £10,

£20 and £50 notes. After Operation *Cicero* was over I learned that nearly all these banknotes were forgeries …

The false notes were so well made that even bank managers fell for them. Our manager in Istanbul was not the only one to be taken in. It was only when they reached the Bank of England, and were examined by the experts of Threadneedle Street, that the truth was finally established.[10]

Sansom and Eppler were both shocked that agents should be given forged currency but it is clear it was near standard procedure within the Abwehr. However, the discovery did confirm Sansom's suspicions that German agents were operating within the city. On his office wall he had a map of the city marked with pins where the forged bank notes had been used, and set up an operation to bring in anybody using Sterling.

Big as the operation was the panic situation in Cairo at the time allowed us to mount it relatively discreetly. It was easy to pretend it was just part of the security measures due to the flap …

We roped in hundreds of people, from British and Allied officers to pimps and shoe-shine boys. Most were indignant, and some – like the flight-sergeant celebrating his birthday with a fiver sent by his aunt – were even innocent, but many were clearly involved in black-marketing, drug-smuggling, robbery, and other crimes, and were very interesting to the Egyptian police. But not to me. Out of all the hours of questioning I did not get a single decent clue.[11]

22. The Raid

SANSOM FINALLY CAUGHT UP WITH Eppler at the Kit Kat Cabaret, a well known haunt of spies. British officers were warned to be tight lipped around the Hungarian dancing girls, and it was even made out of bounds at one time. Sansom saw a grinning Egyptian light a cigarette with a five pound note, and, becoming suspicious, made his move. He ordered a bottle of champagne and joined the group around Eppler uninvited, feigning drunkenness.[1]

'Your birthday, perhaps?' asked Eppler, obviously suspicious of this uninvited intruder and his invitation to help him drink the champagne, notwithstanding the eagerness of the two dancing girls.

'Just a good business deal,' replied Sansom. 'As a matter of fact,' he continued, slurring his words, 'it was a currency transaction – but don't tell anyone.'[2]

Eppler himself does not mention this meeting, perhaps unwilling to admit that he was so easily taken in by Sansom. According to Sansom, he was then introduced to Hekmat Fahmy.

> There was nothing I wanted less. Hekmat Fahmy must have seen me in the Kit Kat many times in uniform as well as in civilian clothes. My dark glasses seemed a shaky disguise.

Eppler introduced himself as Hussein Gaafar and Sandstette as Sandy, who had a strong American accent. At this point Sansom had no idea Eppler was anything but a wealthy Egyptian and a close friend of the famous belly dancer; he was simply following the Sterling which Eppler had burned with such bravado. Fortunately for him, the group invited him back to Hekmat's houseboat for further drinks. All were quite intoxicated, apart from Sansom; the barman at the Kit Kat, Mac, knew to water his drinks.

Two taxis took them down to the Nile, Hekmat and Sansom in the first; he felt he had to make a pass at her under the circumstances, so there followed a clumsy grope, which to his surprise she seemed to enjoy. Or had she been primed by Eppler to try and cultivate this currency dealer?

Once on the boat the talk soon turned to currency exchanges. Sansom had a bite but he stonewalled, advising official channels as the best option; he didn't want to appear too eager. Eppler confided that his friend would rather not take that route, and had about £10,000 to change. They arranged to meet at the Kit Kat the next night.

Sandy went to the agents' own houseboat, apparently to get another bottle of scotch, although Sansom noted that there were several bottles on Hekmat's boat; perhaps Sandy favoured a particular brand. This was how Sansom learned that the two men lived on a nearby boat. Shortly after this Anwar el Sadat appeared, apparently looking for Sandy, and Eppler took him over to the other boat. Sansom began to think he had struck gold.

> All the pieces of the jigsaw began to click into place. It was nearly midnight, and Sandy had invented the excuse about getting more whisky in order to make his nightly broadcast …[3]

Sansom knew who Anwar el Sadat was and that it was more than likely he had come to see the transmitter in action.

Alone with Hekmat, Sansom felt a certain attraction to the dancer, but knew that he had to get off the boat quickly. She no doubt expected another advance. 'Certainly she earned her living by dancing sexily, but that did not mean she was promiscuous, let alone a whore.' More important was that if he made an advance 'I would have to take off my dark glasses, and then she might have recognised me.' His only course of action was to appear severely worse for wear. In the tiny bathroom he made elaborate retching sounds, and emerged wiping sweat off his face, begging for a glass of water. It was 00:15 and still the three men had not returned.

At last they came back. El Sadat 'looked and sounded angry'. Sansom, pleading sickness, left a few minutes later. Finding the nearest telephone he contacted the radio monitoring unit to ask what they had picked up. 'Same as usual,' he was told, which sent him 'dizzily to bed'.[4]

Sansom met with various intelligence officers the next day. The MI6 man 'Bob' did most of the talking. Before them was a clear choice: they could either raid the houseboats right away, or give the spies more time to reveal their network more fully. Picking them up quickly would give them more time to look at the German codes, and they might find vital information on the boats. They might even be able to broadcast misleading information to the Germans. However, if they left it a few days they might be able to round up more of the nest.

Sansom wanted to hold off but Bob was not so sure. If they waited then there was the chance that the agents' nightly transmission would be replied to by the Abwehr. The Abwehr would tell the agents to abort, as they knew that *Kondor*'s contacts (Weber and Aberle) had been captured in May, and that the operation was compromised. Sansom suggested having 'a squad standing by every night at twelve, ready to storm the houseboat at a moment's notice, so that even then we might catch them before they have time to destroy the papers.'

To be doubly sure they could arrange to 'jam' the signal if the Abwehr answered the agents' transmission in order to warn them, although the Abwehr controllers would then write the transmitter and the agents off. There were plainly risks whatever they did, but they decided to consider matters on a day-to-day basis.[5] In the meantime Field Security began arresting some of the contacts the two spies had made, including members of the Swedish Legation. After his arrest Viktor Hauer – the German who had worked at the Swedish Legation – described the houseboat during his interrogation on 24 July:

> The furniture is chintz covered and the woodwork is painted pale green. There are hangings on the canvas walls with decorative Egyptian figure friezes. Between the two flights of steps which lead to the upper deck is a long wooden chest painted pale green. On top of this stands a radio set, in the middle sunk in, is a gramophone turntable, at each end a cupboard. Under the turntable is a sheet of felt which Hauer lifted and found was hiding a Yale lock. It is his belief that the transmitter is hidden there.[6]

Anwar El Sadat and members of the Egyptian forces were left at liberty for fear of alerting Eppler.

Sansom kept his appointment with Eppler that night at the Kit Kat Cabaret, where he changed £100 into Egyptian currency at a reasonable rate, and promised to change more. However, he failed to get an invite to the houseboat as he had wanted, and was told to contact the agents through Hekmat. Sansom had one of his men watching the boat disguised as a beggar, and more men were detailed to tail the two spies as they moved about the city.

It was deemed imprudent to search the houseboat while the two spies were absent, as they would certainly be alerted to the fact by someone. Every night Sansom's men stood ready to raid the boat at midnight, but still of course the spies received no acknowledgement to their messages.

About this time a French cabaret dancer Sansom refers to as Natalie was arrested because she had been seen to spend the night on the spies' houseboat. Mosley calls her Yvette and places her on the houseboat on 27 July; by then she may have been working for Field Security.[7] However this date cannot be correct as Eppler was arrested on 25 July.[8] Dates notwithstanding, Mosley goes on to say that Maurice Hohlman, working for the Jewish Agency in the city, got hold of 'Robby'/'Bob', and they both went to Sansom pleading with him to speak with Yvette as she had uncovered the spies he was looking for, Hohlman even admitting he worked for the Jewish underground and that Yvette worked for him.[9]

According to Sansom, Natalie/Yvette asked to speak to him and one of his NCOs advised him that he should. He found out that she was not French but a Jew from Palestine and she admitted working for a 'Jewish underground organisation'. She and another girl had spent the night with the spies in order to gain information, which they duly did. She had discovered the agents' transmitter hidden in the radiogram, 'big enough for Sandy to get inside when he was transmitting.' She revealed that Sandy had got no reply to the transmission, a fact she had heard him tell Eppler. She also told Sansom that Sandy kept his papers in a book which he kept under his pillow while he slept. That book was *Rebecca*.

Sansom asked her to draw a rough sketch of the houseboat, showing where the two men slept and the location of the radiogram. She apparently volunteered to go back and try and obtain the papers she had seen.[10]

Eppler himself identified the woman as Edith (as opposed to Natalie or Yvette), and was quite taken with her.

> Her eyes were doe-shaped and slanted, her mouth blood-red without
> a touch of make-up. Her eyebrows were perfectly symmetrical arches.
> She had wonderful teeth, like those girls with frozen smiles in tooth-
> paste advertisements.
>
> Her hands were delicate and expressive, her hips shapely and her
> breasts firm and pointed. Her long legs could drive a man wild; her
> skin was soft to the touch and firm all over her body.[11]

Sami the money changer asked Eppler if he really knew Edith; he
said he had met her two months before. Sami claimed that Edith had
been heard to say that Eppler was her lover and that her real employ-
ers were unlikely to work in his best interests. He told him Edith was
working for the terrorist Jewish 'Stern Gang'.

Eppler found this hard to believe and doubted that the Jews could
'afford to dress her in the style she is accustomed to. Have you ever
seen her in the same outfit twice? A wardrobe like hers costs a lot of
money, Sami.'

The money changer laughed at that, and told him the money came
from the British.

For Eppler it then all fell into place: the interest she had shown in
the houseboat. She must be working as an informer for Field Security.
Eppler threatened he would have 'to settle the score with that girl …'[12]

Eppler never got the chance. Field Security moved in on them,
perhaps prompted by Yvette's information that when she had left
them only hours before the two agents had been 'snoring their heads
off' and were 'dead drunk'.[13]

According to Sansom, the raid was fixed for 02:00; he had some
river police seconded to him to effectively surround the craft. The
houseboat was cloaked in darkness as they approached. Something
woke Eppler, some sixth sense.

> The room was pitch dark and the night quite still. Every now and then
> the quiet was broken by the croaking of bullfrogs. The chirping of the
> cicadas in the sycamore trees along the banks of the Nile came in sharp
> little bursts.

There was something wrong. He shot out of bed. 'They were here!
There was a barely perceptible splashing on the water, like fish jump-

ing. But it was not the time of the year when they jumped.' It was the muffled oars of the river police.[14]

Field Security and the police broke down the door; in the darkness something was thrown. Someone called out that it was a grenade and the policemen scrambled for cover. When torches lit up the boat they found the grenade to be a rolled up pair of socks. Eppler stood there naked with a Luger, but seeing the odds against him dropped it.

In Eppler's account of events he mentions the trick they tried with the socks, and states that before the police broke down the door they had removed the bung from the boat's flat bottom in an attempt to scuttle it.

Sandy was caught on deck, but was thought to have thrown something into the Nile. A search of the houseboat failed to find the copy of *Rebecca* or the notes described by Natalie/Yvette/Edith.

> We began tearing the place to pieces, without finding either the book
> or any coded messages. The transmitter was there, all right, hidden in
> the capacious radiogram just as Natalie had said. But that was all.[15]

In fact, the river police were in luck; both the book and the papers had landed in their launch rather than the river. When this was realised Eppler made a grab for the book, but Sansom punched him, making him stagger and fall to the floor. As the two men were taken away, Sansom advised: 'Take my tip and talk, if you want to live.'[16]

Once outside Eppler observed: 'It was still dark and the air pleasantly cool. In the east there was a thin pink line just above the Mogattam Hills. Soon it would be light; another cloudless blue sky would break over Cairo.'[17]

Sansom meanwhile boarded Hekmat Fahmy's boat where she had been arrested. She was furious when she realised who he was. He collected her love letters from admirers in the British forces, some of which contained details of actions and breaches of security. No wonder Eppler had been so interested in her. 'The raid over, I went to bed and slept long and soundly for the first time in weeks.'[18]

Eppler and Sandstette's mission had utterly failed.

23. Rommel at Bay

As all those implicated in the *Kondor* mission were rounded up for interrogation, hundreds of miles to the west the real war rumbled on. Two weeks before the raid on the Nile houseboat, Rommel's Intelligence Service had suffered two other hammer blows.

The Intelligence Service had been extremely useful – if not crucial – in the desert war from the end of May and throughout June, although at times Rommel was inclined to treat it in a cavalier manner. On 1 June Colonel Feller (the 'Good Source') had reported to Washington on the condition of the Eighth Army; almost immediately a copy landed on Rommel's desk.

> June 1 1942 16:43. Personnel losses of the British are fairly light but loss in material heavy. It is estimated that 70% of British tanks engaged were put out of action and at least 50% permanently destroyed. The air ground liaison was poor and the RAF repeatedly bombed own forces.[1]

He also reported on the 'Flap' gripping Cairo, revealing that RAF officers were throwing their files through the windows of offices into trucks waiting below to remove them. This information had gone some way to convincing Rommel to pursue the badly mauled Eighth Army, regardless of earlier plans he had had to halt at the Egyptian frontier. He was willing to risk his vulnerable supply lines in the search of the elusive decisive victory.

At the end of June the 'Good Source' reported British tactical plans. They had initially intended to try and restore the defensive line on the old defences at Mersa Matruh but Auchinleck soon realised that this was not possible and decided that Eighth Army should fall back to the Alamein position. Fellers' reports from Cairo to Washington kept Rommel up-to-date on the British change of plan.[2]

Early in July the 'Good Source' was cut. In May a German POW had told the British of the intercepts, and British code breakers soon broke the US Black Code, and were able to read Fellers' messages an hour after he filed them. Edward Thomas, working at Bletchley Park at the time, felt they learnt about Fellers through Enigma.

> … our suspicions [of Fellers' messages] were aroused through our read-
> ing of Luftwaffe and Panzerarmee Afrika Enigma, and we were finally,
> but somewhat late in the day, able to trace the source of the leak.[3]

Fellers was recalled to Washington, and after that messages contained no useful information. It was a great embarrassment to the US, as their intelligence services had sent a team out to check Fellers' security measures back in the spring, but had given him a clean bill of health. Ironically, later in 1942 Fellers was awarded the Distinguished Service Medal for his work as military attaché, which 'contributed materially to the tactical and technical development of our armed forces.' The citation also stated that 'His reports to the War Department were models of clarity and accuracy.'[4]

The replacement US military attaché in Cairo began using the M-138 strip cipher, which the Axis could not break. Rommel was thus cut off from the strategic intelligence on which he had depended for so long. Hans Otto Behrendt wrote:

> Whatever the reason, from 29 June onwards the Good Source fell
> silent. We no longer had this incomparable source of authentic and
> reliable information, which had contributed so decisively during the
> first half of 1942 to our victories in North Africa.[5]

On 10 July Panzerarmee Afrika had suffered another catastrophe when their 621 Radio Intercept Company was overrun and virtually wiped out. Which in a queer way may have been, partly, a self-inflicted wound. Captain Alfred Seebohm, commander of 621, had apparently been reprimanded by a colonel for not having his unit far enough forward during fighting around Mersa Matruh. That colonel probably had no idea that 621 was not a combat unit 'but a precious and even irreplaceable intelligence gathering operation'.[6]

The criticism, although unjustified, stung the highly strung Seebohm. He knew in early July that his position was far too advanced, only about 6 kilometres west of El Alamein, though he would obtain much better results from there.

The official operations report of the Afrika Korps states:

> Whereas in the south the attack was making good progress and prom-
> ised well for the next day, on 10 July at 06:00 the enemy attacked the
> [Italian] Sabratha division north of the coastal road with a reinforced
> [Australian] brigade after laying down a preparatory artillery barrage
> for one hour with tank support. Italian troops here whose artillery
> seems to have consisted of one light artillery battery and one heavy
> artillery battalion, either surrendered without resistance or took to
> their heels. The Sabratha division was largely wiped out or captured
> and lost its entire artillery except for the heavy battalion. Barely two
> miles south east of the Panzerarmee Command Post itself it was possi-
> ble for us to restore an improvised line of resistance using the machine
> gunners and Flak units attached to the Army headquarters and some
> elements of the 382nd Infantry Regiment which was just arriving
> along the coastal road and keep the enemy from advancing farther.
>
> A regrettable consequence of this route was that the enemy
> advanced so quickly that they were able to destroy nearly the whole of
> 621 Radio Intercept Company.[7]

Colonel Von Mellenthin saw the tragedy unfold as the Sabratha
Division collapsed under the attack of 26th Australian Brigade
and elements of 9th Australian Division, in the Tell el Eisa area.
'Unfortunately the brilliant leader of the listening post service,
Captain Seebohm, fell in this action and most of his important infor-
mation was destroyed or captured.'[8]

It took the British months to go through all the captured codes
and documents, and to question the 101 men captured. One of them
was Seebohm, who was badly wounded. Although taken to a hospital
in Alexandria, he died shortly afterwards. Lieutenant Heinrich Habel
was the last company commander of 621:

> Over the next five or six months several interrogation officers from
> British signals Intelligence did their damnedest to squeeze out of me
> as the last company commander everything they might not yet know.
> Their interrogation methods are well known and there is no need
> to go over them again here. From the questions and remarks of the
> British officers I gained the impression that our working methods and

wireless intelligence successes in North Africa had literally dumb-
founded them, and that afterwards there had been a substantial reshuffle
at the higher levels inside the Corps of Signals.[9]

Thus Rommel, with the crucial August battles coming up, was forced
to rely almost exclusively on air reconnaissance for intelligence; he
could have done with a reliable agent in Cairo. As he had told Eppler
before the agents set off, he wanted to know three facts: 'First, where
will the British make their main stand when I begin my final attack
upon the Delta; second, what reinforcements, in men, tanks and guns,
will they have received; and third, who will lead them?' Now he was
more or less in the dark.[10]

24. Interrogation

WHEN EPPLER AND SANDSTETTE WERE hauled off to the interrogation centre at Maadi neither tried to commit suicide with the standard-issue cyanide capsules, which the Abwehr no doubt had supplied as part of their spy kit. Firstly they were interrogated for three days, 29–31 July.[1] Hassan Gaafar, Father Demetriou, Fatma Amer, Abdel Salama, Hassan Ezzet, Anwar El Sadat and El Masri were all also picked up. They were identified by Eppler, Sandstette and Abdel Rahim, the servant on the houseboat.[2]

Viktor Hauer is often thought to have escaped, however G.J. Jenkins decided to have him kidnapped on 21 July; this was done as he exited a cinema.

> No one saw it and within an hour he was safely hidden in a cell in the newly established interrogation centre at Maadi.
>
> His name was changed to Muller and as far as I am concerned he is an escaped POW picked up on the streets of Cairo and now interned in Palestine. He was thoroughly frightened at his first interrogation and made to understand that his reprieve from shooting was dependent upon his forgetting he was ever called Hauer.
>
> He was thoroughly interrogated and has, I think, told 90% of what he knows.
>
> Both my own police and the Egyptians are still hunting for Hauer whose disappearance was reported by the Swedish Legation.[3]

It is fairly certain that much of the intelligence leading to the arrest of Eppler and Sandstette came from Hauer, rather than from the more colourful Natalie/Yvette/Edith, as related in other accounts. Jenkins may have been overcautious in not bringing Sansom into his confidence, but he was well aware that secrets seldom remained secret for long in Cairo.

Once the two agents were in custody, at least according to Mosley, Monkaster – as he calls Sandstette – botched an attempt at suicide by trying to cut his throat.[4] By the first day the interrogators had their code names of Max and Moritz; this was also confirmed by Hassan Gaafar.

Eppler claims a type of 'good cop, bad cop' system was used on him. A 'burly sergeant' was the 'bad cop', who broke his nose one day, and they also tried drugs on him. Two officers, Major E. Dunston and Captain M.J. Shergold, plied him with cigarettes and cups of tea, claiming they were not the 'Gestapo'. In the end they got something out of him but very little.[5]

However, Eppler's account is contradicted by the Egyptian Military Court of Enquiry into the conduct of El Sadat and Ezzet, which began on 12 August. Ezzet was the first before the court, and the investigating officer opened with the following question:

'In your oath of loyalty to H.M. The King you swore that you would be a friend to his friends and an enemy to his enemies. Great Britain is the ally of Egypt. Do you realise, therefore, that you have broken this oath?'

Ezzet replied, 'I took the oath when I left the Military University and I do not consider that I have broken it.'[6]

He was then asked about all those involved in *Kondor* and his part in it, but denied any knowledge. El Sadat was next up and went through the same process and also denied everything.

On 13 August, Major Dunstan and Sansom sat in on the court proceedings, to which Eppler was brought. He quickly identified Ezzet and Sadat as two of his fellow conspirators. Later Sandstette and Hassan Gaafar were brought in; they both identified Ezzet and El Sadat, who continued to deny any knowledge of events. By this time Eppler and Sandstette may well have done a deal with the British to save their own skins.

A cipher telegram to London identified British concerns:

Eppler and Sandstette originally claimed by us as prisoners of war to get them definitely into our hands and away from Egyptians. They are considered spies, addressed as spies, and themselves admit to being spies.[7]

The whole story of *Kondor* was relayed to the court by various witnesses. On 15 August El Sadat stated that he believed Eppler and Sandstette were lying and trying 'to save their lives'. But little by little El Sadat and Ezzet began to crumble under the weight of evidence, finally admitting knowledge of *Kondor*.

The next day Abdel Salama came before the court. Eppler admitted meeting him at Frau Amer's house, and that he had been interested in creating 'a Gestapo organisation in Egypt', but denied meeting him again claiming he had had no interest in Salama as he could not further his aims.

On 20 August El Masri appeared in court; he too denied ever knowing Eppler, again claiming that the two spies were accusing him to gain favour with the British. The Court of Inquiry closed on that day.

Eppler and Sandstette were kept as political prisoners for the rest of the war, thus avoiding the usual fate of spies. After the war ended they were flown to Germany where they were promptly arrested again as war criminals. MI6 intervened in their case and they were released. Eppler remained in Germany while Sandstette returned to East Africa where he had lived before.

Ezzet and Sadat also avoided execution; they were cashiered from the armed forces and spent two years in prison. El Masri was interned but released before the end of the war on grounds of ill health. Frau Amer, Abdel Salama and Hassan Gaafar were interned for the duration of the conflict. Father Pere Demetriou was deported to Palestine. Hekmat Fahmy was released after a year, while Mohamed Ahmad – the spies' driver – and Albert Wahbo were let off with a warning.

Albert Sansom continued to serve with Field Security and was responsible for security during Winston Churchill's visit in August 1942, who insisted on visiting the front to take a look. As the war progressed west away from Egypt his duties increased in the area of 'protection' for VIPs, Cairo becoming a favourite place for conferences.

The assassination of Lord Moyne, the British Minister of State in the Middle East, in November 1944, shook Sansom. He had warned Lord Moyne that he was a likely target: 'He only laughed. But I still blame myself for having let it happen.'[8] Sansom was first told of the plot by the Zionist Stern Gang by Natalie (Yvette) who he had first met during the *Kondor* case. She sought him out in a night club and told him a political assassination was likely.

Lord Moyne proved stubborn and unwilling to accept protection, not wanting his private life to be invaded by security men. He was gunned down on 6 November while arriving at his house where he had dismissed the guard that morning. His driver, Corporal Fuller, tried to come to his aid and was also murdered by two youths with sub-machine guns, who had been waiting in the portico of the house at Sharia ibn Zanki, near the Gezira sporting club.

Sansom was furious that the report by the guards of their dismissal that morning had not been passed on to him; two hours had passed between their leaving and the assassination. The fact that within minutes the security forces caught the assassins crossing the Boulac Bridge was a hollow victory.

> The trial was very correct and quite short. The accused freely admitted they had killed Lord Moyne. Constable Amin Abdullah gave evidence of their capture.
>
> For security reasons I was not called as a witness. They were found guilty and condemned to death. Neither showed the slightest emotion.[9]

Sansom was selected to be present at the execution in March 1945; 'an unpleasant job if ever there was one.' He found hanging to be 'a filthy business'. He was however impressed by the way the two terrorists met their end.

> As they were positioned on the scaffold they both sang the *Hatikvah*, the Jewish national anthem. Neither finished it. One moment their voices filled the execution chamber, the next, there was absolute silence.[10]

By February 1947 Sansom had swapped his army peak cap for a civilian bowler hat, when he was transferred to the Foreign Office, becoming security officer at the British Embassy in Cairo.

Almásy left North Africa in August 1942 for Athens to get treatment for the amoebic dysentery he had picked up on Operation *Salam*. Before he left, Rommel had turned down his offer to create a German version of the LRDG. Also at this time his friend and possibly lover Entholt returned to the Afrika Korps to serve on Rommel's staff. He must have felt despondent, at the very least.

After treatment in Athens, Almásy decided to go home to Hungary, via Italy and Germany. In Italy he looked up his old friend Pat Clayton, who was a guest of the Italian state in the POW camp at Sulmona in the Abruzzi region. They had a good talk about old times in Egypt before the war, the camp commandant allowing Almásy to take Clayton out of the camp to a bar. There he told Clayton how he had outwitted the LRDG during Operation *Salam*, showing him photographs of the Ford V8 he had used and its modifications.

Some accounts say Pat Clayton 'gritted his teeth' at this. However, according to a biography of Clayton by his son Peter, Pat had a rather different reason for this.

> The remarks about Pat gritting his teeth were more likely to have been due to Almásy's remembered habit, Pat said later, of leaving someone else (Clayton on this occasion!) to pay the bill for the refreshments ordered.
>
> Almásy was nevertheless able to block Pat's transfer to the notorious Campo Cinque, the Italian high security POW camp equivalent of Colditz, and arrange instead for him to go to Campo 29 Veano in Northern Italy … This was appreciated and very much worth the price of a couple of drinks.[11]

Pat Clayton wrote home to his wife Ellie and sister-in-law Nora May, using a code arranged by MI9 for POWs. One letter to his son Peter contained a reference to Peter's little sister 'Dora'. Peter had no sister, and the family sent the letters to the War Office. It was a coded reference to the Abwehr Operation *Dora*, a Brandenburg Regiment scheme to disrupt Allied supply lines in Africa, led by Lieutenant Von Leipzig. The operation was a dismal failure; but Almásy must have mentioned it to Clayton.

In September 1943 Clayton escaped from his POW camp in the confusion as Italy changed sides. He hid in the mountains for many months, but was recaptured in January 1944 and sent to a German POW camp at Marisch-Truban in Czechoslovakia. As the Russians advanced he was moved to Brunswick in Germany, and was liberated there by American troops in April 1945. After the war he continued to serve in the British Army in Palestine and Egypt.

From Abruzzi, Almásy went on to Germany and reported to his Abwehr commander Major Seubert. He requested to be put on the reserve due to his ill health. In Hungary he wrote his memoirs – *With Rommel's Army in Libya* – published in 1943. The book became a bestseller. It was vetted by the Abwehr and 'doctored' by the Nazi Propaganda Ministry, so that there was no direct mention of Operation *Salam* or *Kondor*. However, in chapter eight, 'Desert Patrol', dated May 1942, he describes episodes straight out of *Salam*.[12]

During this time Almásy received the news that Entholt had been killed in action during the retreat from El Alamein, the victim of a land mine. He was desolate, and 'Since then everything has seemed banal, empty and sad.'[13]

Almásy was still on the Abwehr books and in the winter of 1943/1944 he was sent to Turkey, arriving in Istanbul on 5 November; his arrival reported by SIME (Security Intelligence Middle East) later that month.[14] It is likely that he was sent to the city – then a hot bed of intrigue and spies – to work with the pro-German Egyptians there. Abwehr agents there had run Father Demetriou in Cairo and installed the W/T set concealed by the priest in his church for use during Operation *El Masri*. Prince Shahab, of the old Egyptian Khedival family, was one of the main Abwehr agents in Istanbul. Even after the invasion of Sicily in July 1943, Operation *Husky*, the Germans were still concerned with the possible Allied invasion of the Balkans. Thus they were still interested in getting spies into Egypt, the likely starting place for an invasion, and Almásy's expertise was considered of possible use.

About this time Almásy got further involved with Operation *Dora* and the top-secret Luftwaffe unit KG 200 *Kampfgeschunder*. It was set up to carry out special missions under Otto Skorzeny and Walter Schellenberg, the former an Austrian colonel who had led the SS glider team that had rescued Benito Mussolini after he was imprisoned by his own government in 1943.

KG 200 was to set up secret bases in the North African desert to enable aircraft to refuel on long flights behind Allied lines to drop agents. A captured B-17 bomber was used to fly in equipment and technicians to the base. One of the agents was arrested in Freetown and gave the game away. The British and Free French managed to locate the base, although the KG 200 personnel got away. Bletchley Park had also intercepted two messages from Athens mentioning 'Teddy' – one of Almásy's known codenames –indicating the operational area as the Sirte Desert between Cyrenaica and Tripolitania.[15]

By this time the Abwehr was losing its independence, coming more under the control of the unwieldy SS. Almásy more than likely was dismayed by the German occupation of Hungary in March 1944. The Germans had learnt that Admiral Miklos Horthy, the Hungarian dictator, had been making secret peace overtures to the Russians as the Red Army neared the borders of Hungary.

At this stage of the war Hungary had become a refuge for Jews; 750,000 Jews had arrived, many of whom had fled Poland. As the Wehrmacht poured over the border they were followed by the SS, who got to work rounding up the Jews and deporting them to concentration camps. To his credit Almásy saved the lives of several Jewish families, using his rank and reputation as a war hero to bluff his way through awkward situations, and sheltering them at great risk to himself.

In early 1945 Budapest fell to the Red Army in an orgy of rape and looting; thousands of Hungarians were sent to labour camps in Siberia. Almásy was arrested and imprisoned by the NKVD as 'an enemy of the people'. His book *With Rommel's Army in Libya* came back to haunt him, as a demonstration of his complicity with Nazi propaganda. He was subjected to a long, brutal interrogation at notorious 60 Androssy Boulevard in Budapest, the same building that had been used by the Hungarian Fascist Police.

He was questioned for eight months and then put on trial. Many people spoke on his behalf and the charges against him were dropped by the People's Court and he was released. However, in January 1947 he was arrested again, this time by the Hungarian Secret Police, and questioned about his links with western intelligence. It is fairly certain that Alaeddin Moukhton, a cousin of King Farouk, paid a substantial bribe to Almásy's jailers to obtain his release. This was done with the help of MI6, who it appears Almásy was in touch with during the Soviet invasion, sending the British details of Red Army movements.

Travelling under fake papers as Josef Grossman, Almásy moved via the British zone of Austria on to Trieste. There the British consulate supplied him with documents for the onward journey to Rome and then to Cairo.

Almásy just managed to reach the aircraft that would take him to Egypt ahead of the NKVD assassination team who chased his car through the streets of Rome. They had turned up at the front door of his hotel as he slipped out the back door; they were easy to identify in their long overcoats even in the heat of a Roman August. Almásy must have been a British agent at some point and of some importance – even a double agent while still apparently serving the Germans – for MI6 to have gone to such lengths to save his life.[16]

Alaeddin Moukhton and men from British intelligence picked him up at Cairo airport. He was in a bad physical condition, thinner than usual and walking with a stoop. He was set up in a flat in the fashionable Zamalek district of Cairo and paid a small allowance, thankful to be back in his beloved Egypt.[17]

25. The Riddle of Alam Halfa

WHAT WAS THE FATE OF Rommel's Afrika Korps? Following the fall of Tobruk, Rommel felt Egypt was within his grasp. Both armies were like exhausted heavyweight boxers, but he felt if he could land one more decisive blow Egypt must be his. As Desmond Young wrote:

> The Afrika Korps was, indeed, exhausted. But to Rommel, with his tremendous vitality, no soldier was ever too exhausted to fight the last round of a winning battle, or, for that matter, of a losing one.[1]

On 21 June 1942, the day Tobruk fell, Field Marshal Kesselring flew to Africa to discuss matters with Rommel; it had been agreed at the highest level that after the fall of Tobruk the army would halt. Then all available air and sea forces would be turned on Malta, which would later be taken by airborne forces. Rommel argued his advance should continue, and they should not wait for the fall of Malta.

There was rather more to it than a strict choice. Rommel doubted the Italians would ever be ready to invade Malta, but Hitler was expecting the Italians to take a lead role, the Germans having suffered heavy losses during the Battle of Crete.

Count Ciano's diary entry for 20 June demonstrates the indecision in the Italian high command.

> General Carboni has come to Rome to discuss the Malta operation, which has been set for the next new moon. He is convinced, technically convinced, that we are heading for an unheard of disaster. Preparations have been childish; equipment is lacking and inadequate.
>
> The landing troops will never succeed in landing, or, if they land, they are doomed to total destruction.
>
> All the commanders are convinced of this, but no one dares to speak for fear of reprisals by Cavallero [Marshal Ugo Cavallero, Chief of Staff Italian Army]. But I am more than ever of the opinion that the undertaking will not take place.[2]

The momentum was with Rommel and he wanted to go on. On 23 June Ciano wrote in his diary:

> According to some intercepted cables from the American observer at Cairo, Fellers, we learn the English have been beaten and that if Rommel continues his action he has a good chance of reaching as far as the Canal Zone. Naturally, Mussolini is pressing for the attack to continue.[3]

On 21 June Panzerarmee Afrika began pushing east after the retreating British. On that day Rommel was promoted to Field Marshal by Hitler. He confided to his wife Lucie: 'I would much rather he had given me one more division.'[4]

By 24 June they had reached Sidi Barrani and the next day they closed in on Mersa Matruh. That evening General Auchinleck took over direct command of the Eighth Army. He resolved not to defend Mersa Matruh; he could not afford to leave more troops to be bottled up. Rommel struck before the withdrawal was over on 26 June with just 62 tanks and 3000 infantry troops. Auchinleck had decided to try and stop Rommel between Matruh and El Alamein, with 30th Corps occupying the main defences at El Alamein as a precaution.

Rommel's attacking forces took heavy losses in fighting with the New Zealand Division, but his men managed to cut the coast road 20 miles east of Matruh. The British 50th Division and 10th Indian Division fought their way out at night.

The next day Rommel's men reached the El Alamein line at the sea. Alexandria was only 60 miles away. Lieutenant General Fritz Bayerlein confided to Desmond Young, Rommel's biographer, that at that point they had only twelve tanks left.

Then the 'Good Source' dried up, and a few days later Rommel's listening companies were decimated. As Paul Carell observed in his history of the Afrika Korps:

> Now by rights *Kondor* should have been functioning in Cairo. Now the situation had arisen which Almásy had foreseen and feared, and which had made him so eager to deliver Eppler and Sandstette to Cairo. But the Condor's wings had been clipped.[5]

Would it have made any difference if *Kondor* had been set up as planned? It is unlikely in the extreme; Eppler and Sandstette were not dedicated or skilful enough for such a complex mission.

Rommel tried to punch his way through the El Alamein positions, but on 3 July he ordered his soldiers to dig in. 'Every man, from the divisional commanders to the private soldiers, realised that the attack which had begun so victoriously on 26 May and was to end in Alexandria had come to a standstill.'[6]

Limited attacks – some quite heavy – by both sides continued in the first part of of July. Rommel finally went on the defensive on 10 July. On 30 July Auchinleck rightly judged Rommel might attack before the end of August, but where?

At this point Rommel's best option was a withdrawal to a more favourable position, which had the added advantage of shortening his supply lines. However, the German High Command ordered Rommel not to retreat, a political decision. 'They instructed him to stand firm, leaving only one course open to him; to attack; to assemble once more all his forces and gamble everything on a single card.'[7]

It is possible that Rommel's next move – the attack at Alam el Halfa – may have been dictated by a false *Kondor* communication sent by the British. According to Mosley, British intelligence sent a message to German listening stations in Europe and Africa using the code books found with Eppler and Sandstette. After all, all they had to do was 'turn to page 128 of Daphne du Maurier's *Rebecca* and make up their code from the letters in the third paragraph down.'[8]

No doubt the British would have tried this stratagem; it was certainly worth a try. Rommel's radio operators had been told to discount any communication from *Kondor* after the capture of Aberle and Weber. However the Abwehr – after hearing the news of the compromise of *Kondor* – continued to listen on their nets hoping to establish contact via W/T stations in Athens (Adolf) and Libya (Otter). The following order was picked up by Bletchley Park on 7 July.[9]

By order of Schloss [Berlin] *Kondor* is to be called until the end of September and be supervised. Suspension of supervision will be ordered. Transmitting frequencies and call signs of Schildkroete [Weber].

Did the Abwehr listeners 'pick up' a fake British message apparently from *Kondor*, and forward it to Rommel? Mosley certainly thought so.

> *Kondor* calling. Have confirmed message from reliablest source Eighth Army plan to make final stand in battle for Egypt at Alam Halfa. They are still awaiting reinforcements and are not yet ready for more than makeshift defence.[10]

If this message did reach Rommel it could only have come via an Abwehr source.

All this is rather tentative, however one fact stands out: Rommel did attack at Alam el Halfa. However, General Bayerlein, a Colonel at the time and Chief of Staff of the Afrika Korps, tells a rather different story. In his view Rommel had already decided to attack the south of the line, because the British would expect him to strike in the north where the terrain was easier.

Alam el Halfa Ridge lay some fifteen miles behind the centre of the Alamein line and ran south-west to north-east for about twelve miles. It was an ideal backup defensive position against a thrust from the south toward the coast road, and Rommel's men would have to take it.

During the build-up to the attack, a British reconnaissance patrol got lost and strayed into a minefield in the southern sector, where it hit a mine. German troops examining the wreckage found a map case which was rushed up the chain of command.

> The staff were naturally cautious and suspicious. They checked it and made comparisons. 'It's genuine,' was the verdict. Now they had what they needed. The firm *serir* routes were shown and the soft impassable sectors of dunes and drifting sands. Also the treacherous wadis and the broad open patches of desert.[11]

This was a British deception plan, the maps showing a very distorted version of the terrain. Mosley dates this event to 29 August, saying that the dead officer found in the car was a certain

> ... Major 'Smith,' who had dallied with Hekmat Fahmy when he should have been on his way to the desert ... when the Germans went

through the papers of the dead man in the scout car, they found his identity card. His name was Major 'Smith'. They buried him with full military honours.[12]

So where did the dead officer come from, and was he part of the plan?

Sansom also mentions 'a map planted on the Germans, showing the going hard where in fact it was soft sand.' He does not identify any dead British officer.[13]

On 30 August the panzer divisions set off for the southern front with 190 tanks. By this point there had been another change in British command. General Sir Harold Alexander became Commander in Chief Middle East, while General Bernard Montgomery became tactical commander of the Eighth Army.

The Battle for Alam el Halfa is often called the Stalingrad of the Desert. It could also be compared to Gettysburg, where the Confederate commander Robert E. Lee felt he had to batter through for a remote chance of victory as he had no other choice. His Union opponents stood on the defensive, having changed their army commander only a few days before the battle.

For six days the Germans tried to batter through the prepared defences and minefields. Montgomery showed his hand as the Afrika Korps retreated from Alam el Halfa Ridge; there would be no 'loosing of the British armour', no cavalry charge which had lost the British so many tank battles in the past. He would give his wily opponent no opportunity. The Eighth Army would stay 'balanced' and prepare for 'Lightfoot', the second battle of El Alamein.

Maybe the Rebecca Code and Operation *Kondor* did play a part at Alam el Halfa; perhaps it was turned successfully against Rommel. Whatever the truth, it is unlikely we will ever know for sure.

Epilogue

As Eppler and Sandstette languished in prison, on 23 October 1942 Operation *Lightfoot* began, the Second Battle of El Alamein. The British Eighth Army was under the strategic direction of General Sir Harold Alexander and the tactical command of Lieutenant General Bernard Montgomery, who had held back Rommel and the Afrika Korps at Alam el Halfa.

Montgomery now drew the Afrika Korps into a battle of attrition dictated by the positions at El Alamein. There was no way around, no open flank, no room for manoeuvre. The defences on both sides were deep, situated behind large minefields, and the men in both armies were veterans. Montgomery did not want the enemy to retreat; he hoped to destroy them where they stood.

Rommel was well aware of the weakness of his position at the end of a precarious supply line 1500 miles long. To make matters worse, on 23 September he had flown back to Italy and onto Germany on sick leave suffering from a gastric illness, and General Georg Stumme took command.

The Second Battle of El Alamein was marked by Montgomery's philosophy of his army remaining 'in balance'. Thus the battle developed in stages dictated by him, although he was not inflexible; the timetable and direction of attacks could be altered but the stages could not. It started with the 'Break-in' on 23–25 October to clear the minefields; here the timetable was extended by 24 hours.

The 'Dogfight' of 25–31 October required Eighth Army to wear down the Afrika Korps in a mainly infantry fight. By this time Rommel had returned to Africa; Stumme had been killed and command had devolved to General Wilhelm Von Thoma in Rommel's absence.

During the 'Break-out' on 1–4 November Rommel managed to save many of his troops despite Hitler's order not to retreat. The Italians by now were beyond caring, and even the staunch German troops were exhausted. About midday on 4 November the over-stretched Axis defence snapped. Von Thoma was captured while fighting with his escort group. That afternoon Rommel ordered a general withdrawal to save the mobile units of his army. Most of the Italian infantry was abandoned.

The Second Battle of El Alamein was decisive. Rommel had lost half his army and virtually all his tanks; 30,000 of his men were taken prisoner and 20,000 fell in battle. The battle secured the British position in the Middle East, and confirmed that they had found their winning team of Alexander and Montgomery.

The British pursuit was not a great success, partly due to confusion and Montgomery's 'in balance' tactic, and perhaps the magic of Rommel's name played its part. During the long retreat to Tunisia Rommel twice took a stand but on neither occasion would Montgomery take the bait. He stayed 'in balance' at all times, allowing Rommel no opportunity to turn the tables.

Dramatis Personae

Count László Almásy (1895–1951)
A Hungarian adventurer, desert explorer, aviator and motoring enthusiast, who claimed to have found the Zerzura Oasis.

Born in Borostyanko, Hungary, now part of Austria, into a noble family, during the First World War Almásy joined the 11th Hussars Regiment and saw action against the Serbians and the Russians. He transferred to the Austro-Hungarian Air Force in 1916, and was shot down over northern Italy in 1918. He became a flight instructor for the rest of the war.

After the war Almásy became a representative of the Steyr Automobile Company. In 1926 while demonstrating vehicles in Egypt and Sudan, he developed a life-long interest in and love for the desert. In 1932 he took part in an expedition with three Britons, Sir Robert Clayton-East-Clayton, Squadron Leader H.W.G.J. Penderel and Patrick Clayton to find the legendary Zerzura Oasis, 'The Oasis of the Birds'. They found rock art sites in the Gilf Kebir, the 'Cave of the Swimmers'. In 1933 Almásy claimed he had found the third valley of Zerzura.

In 1932 Almásy's former sponsor Clayton-East-Clayton died of an infection picked up on the earlier expedition that year to the Zerzura. His wife, Dorothy died in an air crash a year later in somewhat mysterious circumstances.

In 1935 Almásy may have supplied information to the Italians about the feasibility of an invasion of Egypt and Sudan from Italian North Africa. At the outbreak of the Second World War he returned to Hungary and joined the Hungarian Air Force; later he was recruited by the Abwehr for his extensive desert knowledge and took part in Operation *Salam*, the transportation of two agents from Jalo to Cairo.

After the war he returned to Egypt with the help of MI6. There in 1950 King Farouk made him Technical Director of the Desert Research Institute. He was still obsessed with the prospect of finding the lost army of Cambyses, who according to Herodotus had taken his Persian Army into the desert and promptly disappeared in a sandstorm somewhere between the Farafra Oasis and Bahrein in the Sand Sea. However, his health was failing after years of desert hardship and months of abuse by the Soviet and Hungarian Secret Police.

Within a few weeks of his new appointment he collapsed, and was found to be suffering from hepatitis and amoebic dysentery, which he had first contracted on Operation *Salam*. At the expense of King Farouk he was flown to Austria for treatment at a private clinic near Salzburg. The doctors found that his liver was seriously damaged and neither blood transfusions nor penicillin could much improve his condition. He had no visitors and barely conscious he rambled about Cambyses and the lost army. He died on the afternoon of 22 March 1951. Abu Ramleh, the Father of the Dunes, was buried in the Salzburg municipal cemetery. The only mourners were his doctor, a priest and his brother Janos Almásy and his wife.

Almásy's life, albeit distorted, was propelled into the limelight by the novel *The English Patient*. His grave, which was fast disappearing into obscurity, has now become a shrine with a memorial plaque. A bronze bust of Almásy is now displayed in the grounds of the Hungarian National Geographical Museum at Érd near Budapest.

Brigadier Ralph Bagnold OBE (1896–1990)
A British Royal Engineers/Signals officer, who organised the expeditions in the Libyan Desert in the 1930s and founded the LRDG during the Second World War.

Bagnold and his fellow explorers, including Almásy, were early pioneers in the use of vehicles in the desert. He is credited with developing a sun compass which was not affected magnetically by metal. He helped develop methods of crossing the Sand Seas by reducing tyre pressures and using oversized tyres.

In the early years of the Second World War General Wavell allowed him to create a mobile scouting and raiding force in the desert. In six weeks he formed a new unit which became the LRDG. In 1941, Bagnold was promoted and held a more senior position allowing younger officers to conduct operations.

In June 1944 he retired from the British Army with the rank of brigadier to carry out his scientific research. He continued to study the desert for the rest of his life, and received numerous awards in recognition of his work.

Admiral Wilhelm Canaris (1887–1945)

A German naval officer who became involved with German intelligence operations during the First World War and also commanded a U-boat. In the late 1930s he became head of the Abwehr.

During the Second World War Canaris led a double and charmed life. Right from the start he was set against the Nazis, and had been working against them before the outbreak of war encouraging the British, through links within MI6, to stand up to Hitler.

During the invasion of Poland he was horrified when Hitler ordered him to witness a series of killings carried out by the SS. Amongst these was the burning of the synagogue in Bedzin with its congregation inside. Canaris kept detailed records of this and other incidents in Poland, which found their way to the German resistance. He reported the massacres to General Wilhelm Keitel, who implored him to drop the matter.

Canaris began actively working to overthrow Hitler's regime while seeming to cooperate with it. He was promoted to full admiral in January 1940. During 1942–1943 Canaris made several trips to Spain, during which time he is believed to have made contact with British agents, putting out feelers for peace terms if Hitler could be removed.

However after the invasion of Russia, Operation *Barbarossa*, he began to come under suspicion, particularly by Reinhard Heydrich, head of the SD. The two men had known each other before the war when Heydrich served under Canaris in the navy. Heydrich was an ardent Nazi and was angling to replace Canaris as head of the Abwehr. Canaris called him 'the most impressive of the beasts'. The SD and the Abwehr wasted a great deal of time and effort in plotting against each other. The assassination of Heydrich in Prague in 1942 was partly instigated by MI6 to protect Canaris in his position.

By early 1944 Heinrich Himmler felt that he had enough evidence of Canaris playing a double game and went to Hitler, who dismissed the Admiral. A short time later he was put under house arrest. This prevented him taking part in the July plot of 1944 to kill Hitler.

Himmler kept Canaris alive, hoping to use him in future contacts with the British. However, when it became clear that this was unlikely, Canaris was court-martialled by the SS and sentenced to death. He was executed on 9 April 1945 in Flossenburg concentration camp. He was led to the gallows naked, a final humiliation.

At the Nuremberg Trials many testified to his courage in opposing Hitler. During the war he went out of his way to help those persecuted by the Nazis, saving many Jews by getting them out of Europe via Spain, passing them off as fake Abwehr agents. The Chabad-Lubavitch organisation campaigned for his recognition as a Righteous Gentile.

Patrick Clayton DSO MBE (1896–1962)
A British surveyor and desert explorer, who led the first LRDG raid.

Clayton was a pre-war desert explorer along with Ralph Bagnold. He spent eighteen years with the Egyptian Government Survey. In 1931 he helped rescue Sanusi refugees from Italian troops who had occupied Kufra. He often acted as a guide for tourists on desert trips and in 1937 rescued the German Defence Minister who apparently got lost in the area, although more than likely the man was on a reconnaissance mission.

Bagnold sent for Clayton to help form the LRDG when he was commissioned into the Intelligence Corps. He was wounded and captured on the first LRDG operation of the war in 1941, spending the rest of the conflict in POW camps.

After escaping a POW camp at Veano in northern Italy he lived in the mountains for four months, but was recaptured in January 1944 and sent to a prison camp in Czechoslovakia and then on to Germany. He was soon on the camp escape committees, compiling maps and documents for escapees. It was dangerous work, and he later told the story of two friends caught by the Gestapo who were returned to the camp for burial in urns.

On 12 April 1945 he was liberated at Oflag 79 by US troops. When Peter his son met him at the station he only recognised his father by his LRDG shoulder flashes. He was thin and worn out by four years of bad diet and ill treatment in the camps.

After the war Clayton stayed in the army serving in Palestine and Egypt. In 1950 with his wife Ellie he attended the celebration of the Desert Institute in Cairo, where he met old members of the Zerzura Club, including Bagnold and Almásy.

After 30 years spent in the Middle East mapping the deserts, he returned home in 1953. Clayton continued working as a reserve officer until the year before his death in 1962. He was used as the inspiration for Peter Madox in *The English Patient*.

Daphne du Maurier, Lady Browning (1907–1989)
British author.

Daphne du Maurier, author of *Rebecca*, has become one of the best loved of British novelists. She was the second of three daughters of the actor manager Sir Gerald du Maurier. Her grandfather George du Maurier had himself written three novels, *Trilby* (1894) being the most famous.

Daphne's first novel *The Loving Spirit* was published in 1931. Her most famous books were set in her adopted Cornwall. *Rebecca* was published in 1938 and is generally regarded as her finest work, adapted for stage and screen numerous times. The film of the book directed by Alfred Hitchcock won the Best Picture Oscar in 1941.

Notwithstanding the success of *Rebecca*, many critics believe her macabre short stories were her best work, including *The Birds* (1963) and *Don't look Now* (1973), both of which were adapted for the screen. *Rebecca* and most of her other books remain in print to this day.

Daphne married Frederick Browning in 1932, later to become Lieutenant-General Sir Frederick Browning, who died in 1965. Daphne died at her home in Cornwall in 1989. Her son Christian (Kit) Browning still lives at the family house, 'Ferryside', near Fowey.

John Eppler, alias Johannes Eppler, alias Hussein Gaafar (1914–?)
German/Egyptian Abwehr spy.

After Eppler was arrested in July 1942, he was put through a court martial and sentenced to death, the fate awaiting most spies. However, in view of the volatile political situation in Egypt and his willing cooperation with his captors, both Eppler and his accomplice Sandstette were treated as political prisoners.

He was held in prison until the autumn of 1946, when he was flown to Germany. There he was interned at Hamburg-Neuenganme in a camp for war criminals, but MI6 intervened and he was released.

He then began working in the black market, at which time, according to Eppler himself, the KGB contacted him to spy for them, but he turned them down. Life became too 'hot' so he moved to the rural south of Germany to Saarland, where his mother had come from, and started a book business.

In 1957 Eppler moved to France. In 1974 he wrote his memoirs while living in a flat in Paris on the banks of the Seine. In 1980 Pamela Andriotokis interviewed him for *People* magazine, after the release of Ken Follett's novel *The Key to Rebecca*, Then 66, Eppler was living outside Paris in an apartment near Versailles, a wealthy business man.

'Lili Marlene'

A German love song the fictional character of which became the distant sweetheart of all the men of the desert armies.

While serving in the Imperial German Army in 1915, a school teacher called Hans Leip wrote a poem that would become the basis of the famous song. It was published in 1937 as 'The Song of a Young Soldier on Watch'. It was then set to music by Norbert Schultze in 1938 and released under the title 'The Girl under the Lantern'. It was first recorded by Lale Andersen in 1939.

Joseph Goebbels, the Nazi propaganda minister, tried to stop the song being broadcast saying that it was too 'sentimental'. The outcry from Axis soldiers, including Erwin Rommel himself, was too great and Goebbels changed his mind. It was these troops who gave the song its popular name 'Lili Marlene'. Eventually all the desert armies were tuning into Radio Belgrade to hear it.

In 1944 Marlene Dietrich recorded the song for the US Office of Strategic Services musical propaganda broadcasts.

Underneath the lantern
By the barrack gate,
Darling I remember
The way you used to wait
T'was there that you whispered tenderly
That you loved me;
You'd always be
My Lili of the lamplight
My own Lili Marlene

English lyrics by Tommie Connor, 1944

Leonard Mosley (1913–1992)
British war correspondent and author.

Mosley was a journalist and war correspondent for *The Sunday Times*. It was while serving in this capacity in the Middle East that Mosley first came across Eppler and the story of Operation *Kondor*.

His job soon took him away from the region as the war moved toward Europe. He parachuted into Normandy on D-Day with the 6th British Airborne Division, and reported on the final collapse of the Nazi regime in 1945. However, he never forgot Eppler and tracked him down in Germany in 1956. Subsequently they met several times; on occasion Eppler visited Mosley in his Surrey home. The result was *The Cat and the Mice* (1958), a somewhat distorted account, but it did bring Operation *Kondor* into the public arena.

Later Mosley became a renowned biographer, his subjects including General George Marshal, Reichmarschall Herman Goring, Walt Disney and Charles Lindbergh, amongst others. He also wrote five novels.

Lieutenant-Colonel Nikolaus Ritter (1897–?)
German Abwehr officer and agent

At the end of the war Ritter was serving in a Luftwaffe flak regiment as the Abwehr had collapsed. He was captured by MI6 and questioned for a year at various POW camps.

He was told that many of the agents he had run during the war had in fact been double agents, run by the British, a fact that he claimed to refuse to believe at first. His captors knew his various cover names, including Doktor Rantzau – he was fond of being a Doktor – Jansen, Reinhardt and Alfred Harding.

It appears that whatever Ritter told the British, he did, at least at one time, have an inkling of the Allied 'Double Cross System'. Gwilyn Williams, a Welsh nationalist codenamed 'Snow', was an Abwehr agent turned by MI6. Ritter, in his cover as Dr Rantzau, saw Williams in Lisbon in 1941 and accused him of being a double agent (Snow KV 4/444–453). Ritter's superiors did not agree and Snow was sent back to England on another mission, but his British controllers decided to wind down the operation.

Later Ritter worked for the CIA in Europe. He was last heard of living at Gross Flottbek on the River Elbe near Hamburg.

Field Marshal Erwin Rommel (1891–1944)

'The Desert Fox', an inventive tactical commander, especially in mobile battle, although his strategic ability and administrative skills were questionable.

Rommel was born in Heidenheim near Ulm. He joined the German Army in 1910, completing his officer training at Danzig in 1911. He was commissioned lieutenant in January 1912. During the First World War Rommel fought in France, Romania and Italy in the 6th Wurttemberg Infantry Regiment and the Wurttemberg Mountain Battalion. He was wounded three times. On 27 November 1916 he married Lucie (Lucia Maria Mollin), to whom he was devoted. Their son Manfred was born on 24 December 1928. In the inter-war period he became an instructor at the Dresden Infantry School, where he wrote a book on infantry tactics: *Combat Tasks for Platoon and Company: A Manual for Officer Instruction*.

During the 1939 invasion of Poland, Rommel commanded the Führer Escort Headquarters. In February 1940, through Hitler's patronage, he was given command of the 7th Panzer Division for the invasion of France; he received both praise and criticism for his actions, some observers finding him bold and inventive while others considered him reckless.

In 1941 he was given command of German forces in North Africa, Panzerarmee Afrika, later becoming the Afrika Korps. His object was the capture of Egypt and the Suez Canal. The war rolled back and forth across the Libyan and Egyptian deserts. Rommel's advance was finally stopped at the First Battle of El Alamein. At Alam el Halfa he tried to batter his way through well prepared British positions but had to withdraw.

At the Second Battle of El Alamein the Afrika Korps was in a desperate situation but Hitler refused permission to retreat, which Rommel accepted with misgivings. Hitler later rescinded the order.

The retreat from El Alamein continued for 1500 miles apart from brief rearguard actions all the way to Tunisia, against a vastly superior Allied force that had air supremacy. In February 1943 Rommel inflicted a heavy defeat on the US II Corps at the Kasserine Pass. In March, due to ill health, he handed over command of Armeegruppe Afrika to General Hans-Jurgen Von Arnim and left for Germany, never to return to Africa.

In July Rommel took command of Army Group E to defend Greece against possible Allied landings. With the overthrow of Mussolini he went to Italy to command Army Group B. When Field Marshal Albert Kesselring took command in Italy, Rommel went to France with Group B, his instructions being to prepare the defence against Allied invasion. Although most of the German commanders, including Hitler, believed that the Allies would land in the Pas-de-Calais, Rommel thought it more likely they would land in Normandy. His view was that the invasion should be stopped on the beaches, because Allied air superiority would expose large movements of troops to heavy punishment. In contrast, Field Marshal Gerd Von Runstedt thought that the heavy German mobile reserves should be held further back in a position from where a more traditional counter attack could be launched. Hitler vacillated between the two plans but picked neither, instead placing the reserves farther forward, but not close enough for Rommel or far enough back for Von Runstedt. Rommel was on leave when the D-Day landings began. He returned to the front and on 17 July his staff car was strafed by a Spitfire. Rommel was wounded and hospitalised.

Rommel was indirectly implicated in the 20 July plot against Hitler, in which some of his closest friends were involved. However he himself held the view that Hitler should not be assassinated but rather arrested. He was given the choice of facing the People's Court or committing suicide. Knowing that the former almost certainly meant execution and that his family would be badly treated, he chose the latter. On 14 October 1944 he took cyanide and ended his life. The official Nazi line was that he had died of a heart attack brought on by his wounds. He was buried, against his wishes, with all the pomp the Nazi state could muster.

Many soldiers and military historians believe it was Rommel's skilful use of desert terrain that cemented his reputation. As Winston Churchill said in a speech to the Houses of Parliament, 'We have a very daring and skilful opponent against us, and, may I say across the havoc of war, a great general.'

Heinrich Gerd Sandstette, alias Peter Monkaster (1913–?)
German Abwehr spy.

Sandstette was born in Oldenburg and educated in Germany, where he lived until 1930. That year he went to West Africa, going on to work in several African countries until the outbreak of the Second World War. He was repatriated to Germany in 1940 as part of an exchange of British and German civilians. With his African background he was chosen for Operation *Kondor* while working in the Abwehr map department.

When Eppler and Sandstette (nicknamed Sandy by Eppler) were captured in Cairo and imprisoned he tried to cut his throat but botched the job, and spent several weeks in hospital.

Like Eppler, at the end of the war Sandstette was flown back to Germany. Finally obtaining release from a camp for war criminals, he returned to East Africa and took up farming.

Major A. W. Sansom MBE (1909–1973)
A British insurance salesman who served in the Field Security Service (Intelligence Corps) for most of the Second World War.

After the arrest of Eppler and Sandstette in 1942 – the high point of Sansom's career – he continued to serve in Cairo as a security officer. He dealt with a variety of factions, from Egyptian nationalists wishing to cast off the British imperialist yoke, to mutinies within the Greek forces then serving in Egypt that heralded the civil war in Greece. He was also faced with the machinations of various Zionist groups who had their eye on Palestine.

After the war Sansom was appointed as security officer in the British Embassy, Cairo. In July 1952 the Egyptian Army took over the government. Anwar el Sadat became the First Minister of State in the revolutionary Egyptian government and King Farouk was deposed as head of state.

Sansom had to leave in a hurry, given his background of having arrested most of the leading revolutionaries during the war years, who had openly vowed revenge. He returned home to England, a country he had spent little time in. He had to learn to live without his luxury flat and servants in an austere post-war Britain, but his service to the nation was recognised with the award of the MBE recorded in the New Year's honours list for 1953.

In 1960 Sansom met Eppler again in London at a reception for the premiere of the film *Foxhole in Cairo*. In 1965 he published his memoir, *I Spied Spies*.

The details of Sansom's last days are not clear. However, there is an Alfred William Sansom, apparently born in Egypt, buried at the Ta' Braxia cemetery in Malta. His date of death is given as 19 February 1973. Did Sansom spend his last years on the sunny island of Malta? It is to be hoped, for if there is one hero in this story surely it is 'Sammy' Sansom.

Notes

The Following abbreviations have been used:

Foreign Office	(FO)
Government Code and Cypher School Files Bletchley Park	(GCCS)
Imperial War Museum	(IWM)
Lloyd Owen papers	(LOP)
Security Service Files	(KV)
Public Record Office	(PRO)
War Office	(WO)

Prologue

1 Forster, M., *Daphne du Maurier* p.127–128

2 Sansom, A.W., *I Spied Spies* p.11

3 Du Maurier, D., *The Loving Spirit* p.191

Chapter 1: Johannes Eppler, Beirut May 1937

1 Denham, H.M., *Southern Turkey the Levant and Cyprus* p.70

2 KV/2/1467 small moustache, light coloured eyes

3 Eppler, J., *Operation Condor Rommel's Spy* p.31

4 Mosley, L., *The Cat and the Mice* p.16

5 Eppler, p.32

6 ibid, p.37

7 ibid, p 42

8 ibid, p.49

Chapter 2: Eppler, Athens and Berlin, July–August 1937

1 Eppler, p.50–54

2 ibid, p.55

3 ibid, p.57–61

4 Davies, N. *Heart of Europe: A Short History of Poland* p.369

5 Jorgensen, C., *Hitler's Espionage Machine* p.26

6 Bassett, R., *Hitler's Spy Chief* p.67

7 ibid, p.43

8 Jorgensen, p.43

9 Bassett, p.53–57

10 Andrew, C., *Secret Service* p.115

11 Bassett, p.59

12 Jorgensen, p.25

13 Bassett, p.250

14 Jorgensen, p.26
15 Eppler, p.62
16 Bassett, p.65
17 Eppler, p.62–63
18 p.62–63
19 Eppler, p.65–69

Chapter 3: László Almásy
1 Bierman, J., *The Secret Life of László Almásy* p 18
2 ibid, p.253
3 Cooper, A., *Cairo in the War 1939–1945* p.204
4 Bierman, p 131
5 ibid, p.128
6 KV/2/1467 bitter personal glory
7 Carell, P., *The Foxes of the Desert* p.205
8 Rawlinson, G., *Herodotus* p.426

Chapter 4: Alfred Sansom
1 Sansom, A.W., *I Spied Spies* p.11
2 Cooper, p.36
3 Sansom, p.12–14
4 ibid, p.22
5 ibid, p.29–31
6 ibid, p.36
7 Pitt, B., *The Crucible of War Wavell's Command* p 120

Chapter 5: Cairo, Spring 1941
1 Sansom, p.45
2 Pitt, p.241
3 Sansom, p.40
4 Cooper, p.115
5 Stark, F., *Dust in the Lion's Paw* p.60
6 Pick, C., *Egypt a Traveller's Anthology* p.95
7 Forster, p.128–129
8 Pick, p.79
9 ibid, p.81–82
10 Sansom, p.49
11 Playfair, Major-General I.S.O., *The Mediterranean & Middle East* Volume 1 p.377
12 ibid, p.389

Chapter 6: The Western Desert
1 KV/2/1467 p.5
2 Cooper, p.110
3 Neillands, R., *Eighth Army* p.3

4   Bierman, p.142
5   Pitt, p.223
6   Playfair (Volume 1), p.295
7   Bagnold, R., *Sand, Wind and War* p.219
8   Playfair, (Volume 1), p.295
9   Kennedy Shaw, W.B., *Long Range Desert Group* p.24–25
10 ibid, p.42
11 Clayton, p.153
12 ibid, p.147

Chapter 7: Tripoli, March 1941

1   Lewin, p.32
2   Carell, p.6
3   Farago, L. *The Game of the Foxes* p.40–41
4   Whiting, p.34
5   Carell, p.13
6   Bierman, p.132
7   Sebag-Montefiore, H., *Enigma* p.129
8   KV 2/87
9   Sansom, p.77
10 KV/2/1467

Chapter 8: The Troublesome General

1   Sansom, p.57
2   Eppler, p.147
3   Playfair, Major-General I.S.O., *The Mediterranean & Middle East Volume 2* p.178
4   ibid, p.179
5   ibid, p.179
6   Cooper, p.69
7   Playfair (Volume 2), p.185
8   Ritter, N., *Deckname Dr Rantzau* p.406–407
9   Bierman, p.154
10 Sansom, p.72–74
11 Cooper, p.71
12 PRO WO 208/1560, 22/5/1941
13 Kelly, S., *The Lost Oasis* p.169
14 Sansom, p.76
15 Eppler, p.177
16 Christie, A., *Agatha Christie: An Autobiography* p.383
17 Eppler, p.179–180
18 Playfair (Volume 2), p 183–184
19 ibid, p.196
20 ibid, p.197
21 Eppler, p.183

Chapter 9: Exit Ritter

1 GCCS No 5798 Ritter to Hamburg 27/5/1941
2 Carell, p.207
3 ibid, p.208
4 Bierman, p.156
5 Carell, p.209
6 ibid, p.208–210
7 Whiting, C., *Hitler's Secret War* p.71
8 Carell, p.210–211
9 GCCS No 6801 Cyrenaica to Berlin 20/6/1941
10 Whiting, p.71
11 Ritter, p.450
12 GCCS No 8920 Berlin to Cyrenaica 27/6/1941
13 KV/2/1467 So/I/0842
14 KV/2/1467 Ford V8 Lorries

Chapter 10: Under the Pagoda Tree

1 Andrew, p.449
2 Simmons, M., *The Battle of Matapan 1941* p.30
3 ibid, p.148–149
4 Pitt, p.249
5 Connell, J., *Wavell Supreme Commander* p.385–386
6 ibid, p.386
7 Pitt, p.252
8 Liddell Hart, B.H., *The Rommel Papers* p.104
9 Behrendt, H.O., *Rommel's Intelligence in the Desert Campaign* p.52–53
10 Liddell Hart, p.111
11 Playfair (Volume 2), p.29
12 Cooper, p.67
13 Pitt, p.275
14 Playfair (Volume 2), p.41
15 ibid, p.156
16 Connell, p.20

Chapter 11: The 'Good Source'

1 Stark, F., *East is West* p.130
2 Sansom, p.81
3 ibid, p.88–89
4 Eppler, p.184
5 ibid, p.187
6 ibid, p.189–192
7 Kahn, D., *The Codebreakers* p.250
8 Ranfurly, Countess, H., *To War with Whitaker* p.78
9 *World War II Magazine* June 2006
10 Kahn, p.248–249

11 Ciano, Count, G., *Ciano's Diary 1937–1943* p.450
12 Behrendt, p.146
13 Kahn, p.251
14 Moorehead, A., *African Trilogy* p.180
15 Neillands, p.77

Chapter 12: Interview with the Führer
1 KV 2/88
2 Jorgensen, p.179
3 Eppler, p.194
4 ibid, p.194–195
5 Documents on German Foreign Policy p.881
6 Bullock, A., *Hitler a Study in Tyranny* p.614
7 Eppler, p.195
8 Mosley, L., *The Cat and the Mice* p.28–29
9 Eppler, p.196–197

Chapter 13: Planning
1 KV 3/5 MI5 Memo
2 Eppler, p.199
3 Kelly, p.200
4 KV 3/5 MI5
5 Eppler, p.209
6 GCCS 19/94 No 26386 Berlin-Tripoli 20/2/1942
7 GCCS 19/28 No 25064 Berlin-Tripoli 16/4/1942
8 Bletchley Park National Codes Centre
9 Bierman, p.169
10 Carell, p 48
11 Cooper, p.146
12 Lewin, R., *Rommel as Military Commander* p.96

Chapter 14: The Rebecca Code
1 KV 3/3 No 25357 Berlin to Tripoli 24/3/1942
2 Almásy, L., *With Rommel's Army in Libya* p.56
3 ibid, p.56
4 ibid, p.58
5 ibid, p.56
6 Bierman, p.160
7 Almásy, p.46
8 ibid, p.64
9 Whiting, p.72
10 Almásy, p.60
11 Whiting, p 72–73
12 Carell, p.213
13 Whiting, p.72–73
14 Almásy, p.60

15 Brown, A.C., *Bodyguard of Lies* p.105–109
16 Willmore, A., Bookends of Fowey
17 Book & Magazine Collector No 285 September 2007

Chapter 15: False Start 99

1 GCCS 19/94 No 26524 *Salam* message
2 Eppler, p 198–200
3 ibid, 202–203
4 ibid, p.203
5 Almásy, p.79
6 ibid, p.81–82
7 Almásy, p 92–94
8 GCCS 19/28 No 25061 Tripoli to Berlin 15/4/1942
9 Kelly, p.202
10 Carell, p.216–217
11 KV/2/1467 ref 50/I/0842
12 GCCS 19/30 No 28316 Salam-Western Desert area 8/5/1942
13 Eppler, p.203
14 GCCS 19/30 No 28341 Salam-Western Desert area G2 13/5/1942
15 IWM-LOP *Operation Salam Diary*
16 Behrendt, p.57
17 GCCS 19/30 No 28337 Salam-Western Desert area G2 4/5/1942

Chapter 16: Operation Salam

1 IWM-LOP *Operation...* p.2
2 ibid, p.10
3 ibid, p.2
4 Kelly, p.205
5 IWM-LOP *Operation...* p.3
6 ibid, p.3
7 ibid, p.4
8 Eppler, p.208
9 IWM-LOP *Operation...* p.4
10 Almásy, p.96
11 Eppler, p.207
12 ibid, p.208–209
13 IWM-LOP *Operation...* p.5
14 Eppler, p.209
15 IWM-LOP *Operation...* p.6
16 GCCS 19/32 No 30887 18/5/1942
17 IWM-LOP *Operation...* p.6
18 ibid, p.8
19 Almásy, p.97
20 IWM-LOP *Operation...* p.9
21 Eppler, p.209
22 Almásy, p.98

23 IWM-LOP *Operation...* p.9
24 ibid, p.10
25 IWM-LOP *Operation...* p.12
26 Eppler, p.212
27 ibid, p.214

Chapter 17: Assiut
1 KV/2/1467 Appendix A
2 ibid, Appendix D
3 Eppler, p.215
4 IWM-LOP *Operation...* p.10
5 Eppler, p.216
6 ibid, p.217
7 Bierman, p.184

Chapter 18: The Flap
1 Carell, p.159
2 Landon, C., *Ice Cold in Alex* p.1
3 Neillands, p.131
4 Playfair, Major-General I.S.O., *The Mediterranean & Middle East Volume 3* p.274
5 Carell, p.199
6 Ranfurly, p.134
7 Cooper, p.193
8 Sansom, p.96
9 ibid, p.97
10 Eppler, p.218
11 ibid, p.226
12 Sansom, p.96
13 ibid, p.100–101
14 KV/2/1467 16A
15 Sansom, p.103–104
16 ibid, p.106–107

Chapter 19: Kondor Calling
1 KV/2/1467 6A p.4
2 ibid, p.5
3 Kelly, p.221
4 KV/2/1467 13A p.2
5 ibid, 6A p.5
6 Eppler, p.220–221
7 Sansom, p.119
8 Eppler, p.221
9 KV/2/1467 6A p.5
10 Eppler, p.225
11 KV/2/1467 13A para 6

12   ibid, 6A p.5
13   Eppler, p.225–226
14   ibid, p.238
15   IWM LOP *Operation...* p.13
16   ibid, p.13
17   ibid, p.17
18   ibid, p.16
19   ibid, p.17
20   ibid, p.18
21   ibid, p.20
22   GCCS 19/31 No 29397 Berlin to Tripoli 8/6/1942
23   Carell, p.221
24   Behrendt, p.153
25   Carell, p.222

Chapter 20: The Ring Tightens
1   KV/2/1467 ref40
2   Mosley, p.85
3   Sansom, p.117
4   Jeffery, K. *MI6* p.427
5   Mosley, p.89
6   KV/2/1467
7   Sansom, p.118
8   KV/2/1467 Appendix D
9   ibid, Appendix A p.2
10   ibid, 13A
11   Eppler, p.222
12   ibid, p.223
13   KV/2/1467 13A p.2
14   Eppler, p.230
15   KV/2/1467 (Letter to His Excellency)
16   FO 141/852 Jenkins to Tamlyn 2/8/1942
17   KV/2/1467 17A Appendix A p.2
18   ibid, p.2
19   ibid, p.3
20   ibid, p.3
21   KV 3/5 p.70
22   Sadat, A., *Revolt on the Nile* p.47
23   Eppler, p.232–233

Chapter 21: Currency Matters
1   KV/2/1467 13A p.2
2   Cooper, p.37
3   Sansom, p.113
4   ibid, p.113
5   KV/2/1467 13A Part II p.1

6   Sansom, p.114
7   ibid, p.115
8   Eppler, p.234
9   Jorgensen, p.110
10 Moyzisch, L.C., Operation *Cicero* p.202–203
11 Sansom, p.116–117

Chapter 22: The Raid
1   Cooper, p.123
2   Sansom, p.119
3   ibid, p.120
4   ibid, p.123
5   ibid, p.124–126
6   KV/2/1467 Interrogation of Viktor Hauer 24/7/1942
7   Mosley, p.114
8   KV/2/1467
9   Mosley, p.126
10 Sansom, p.129
11 Eppler, p.235
12 ibid, p.237
13 Mosley, p.128
14 Eppler, p.238
15 Sansom, p.131
16 ibid, p.131
17 Eppler, p.240
18 Sansom, p.132

Chapter 23: Rommel at Bay
1   Behrendt, Appendix II p.233
2   ibid, p.166
3   ibid, p.167
4   Kahn, p.255
5   Behrendt, p.167
6   ibid, p.170
7   ibid, p.168
8   Carell, p.242–243
9   Behrendt, p.172–173
10 Mosley, p.75–76

Chapter 24: Interrogation
1   KV/2/1467 ref 40
2   ibid.
3   ibid, Jenkins to Sir David Petrie MI5 1/8/1942
4   Mosley, p.141
5   ibid, p.142
6   KV/2/1467 16A

7   ibid, Telegram No 532 Cairo-London
8   ibid, 20/8/1942 p.2
9   Sansom, p.166
10 ibid, p.181
11 ibid, p.181–182
12 Clayton, P., *Desert Explorer* p.156
13 Almásy, p.96
14 Bierman, J., *The Secret Life of László Almásy* p.201
15 WO 208/1562 SIME No157 22/11/1942
16 GCCS 19/66 No 7568 Athens-Berlin 13/2/1944
17 Kelly, p.251

Chapter 25: The Riddle of Alam Halfa

1   Young, D., *Rommel the Desert Fox* p.140
2   Ciano, p.530
3   ibid, p.531
4   Young, p.142
5   Carell, p.227
6   ibid, p.241
7   ibid, p.251
8   Mosley, p.147
9   GCCS 19/38 No 38789 Athens to Libya 6/7/1942
10 Mosley, p.148
11 Carell, p.254–255
12 Mosley, p.151
13 Sansom, p.132

Bibliography

Almásy, László, *With Rommel's Army in Libya* (1st Books Library, 2001)

Andrew, Christopher, *Secret Service* (Heinemann, 1985)

Asher, Michael, *Get Rommel* (Weidenfeld & Nicolson, 2004)

Bagnold, Ralph A., *Sand, Wind and War* (University of Arizona Press, 1990)

Bassett, Richard, *Hitler's Spy Chief* (Weidenfeld & Nicolson, 2005)

Behrendt, Hans-Otto, *Rommel's Intelligence in the Desert Campaign* (William Kimber, 1980)

Bierman, John, *The Secret Life of László Almásy* (Viking, 2004)

Boleman-Herring, Elizabeth, *Vanishing Greece* (Parkway Publishing, 2003)

Brendon, Piers, *The Dark Valley a Panorama of the 1930s* (Jonathan Cape, 2000)

Brown, Anthony Cave, *Bodyguard of Lies* (Harper & Row, 1975)

Bullock, Alan, *Hitler a Study in Tyranny* (Odhams Press, 1953)

Carell, Paul, *The Foxes of the Desert* (Macdonald, 1960)

Christie, Agatha, *An Autobiography* (Collins, 1977)

Ciano, Count Galeazzo, *Ciano's Diary 1937–1943* (William Heinemann, 1947)

Clayton, Peter, *Desert Explorer* (Zerzura Press, 1998)

Cooper, Artemis, *Cairo in the War 1939–1945* (Hamish Hamilton, 1989)

Cooper, John, *The Queen's Agent Francis Walsingham at the Court of Elizabeth I* (Faber and Faber, 2011)

Connell, John, *Wavell Supreme Commander* (Collins, 1969)

Davies, Norman, *Heart of Europe: A Short History of Poland* (Oxford University Press, 1986)

Deighton, Len, *City of Gold* (Century, 1992)

Denham, H.M., *Southern Turkey the Levant and Cyprus* (John Murray, 1973)

Du Maurier, Daphne, *The Loving Spirit* (Heinemann, 1931)

_____ *Rebecca* (Victor Gollancz, 1938)

Eames, Andrew, *The 8.55 to Baghdad* (Bantam Press, 2004)

Eppler, John, *Operation Condor Rommel's Spy* (Macdonald and Jane's, 1977)

Farago, Ladislas, *The Game of the Foxes* (David McKay, 1971)

Fisher, David, *The War Magician* (Weidenfeld & Nicolson, 2004)

Follett, Ken, *The Key to Rebecca* (Hamish Hamilton, 1980)

Foot, M.R.D. & Langley, J.M., *MI9 Escape and Evasion 1939–1945* (The Bodley Head, 1979)

Forster, Margaret, *Daphne du Maurier* (Chatto & Windus, 1993)

Frankland, Nobel & Dowling, Christopher (eds), *Decisive Battles of the Twentieth Century* (Sedgwick & Jackson, 1976)

Haining, Peter, *The Mystery of Rommel's Gold* (Robson Books, 2004)

Heckstall-Smith, Anthony, *Tobruk* (Anthony Blond, 1959)

Jorgensen, Christer, *Hitler's Espionage Machine* (Lyons Press, 2004)

Kahn, David, *The Codebreakers* (Weidenfeld & Nicolson, 1974)

Kelly, Saul, *The Lost Oasis* (John Murray, 2002)

Kennedy, Shaw, *Long Range Desert Group* (Greenhill Books, 1990)

Landon, Christopher, *Ice Cold in Alex* (William Heinemann, 1957)

Lewin, Ronald, *Rommel as Military Commander* (B.T. Batsford, 1968)

Liddell Hart, B.H. (ed), *The Rommel Papers* (Collins, 1953)

Macintyre, Ben, *Agent Zig Zag* (Bloomsbury, 2007)

Mack, J.E., *A Prince of our Disorder. The Life of T.E. Lawrence* (Little Brown & Company, 1976)

McKay, Sinclair, *The Secret Life of Bletchley Park* (Aurum Press, 2010)

Manley, Deborah, *The Nile a Traveller's Anthology* (Cassell, 1991)

Minghella, Anthony, *The English Patient a Screenplay* (Methuen Drama, 1997)

Montagu, Ewen, *Beyond Top Secret Ultra* (Coward, McCann & Geoghegan, 1978)

Moorehead, Alan, *African Triology* (Hamish Hamilton, 1944)

Morgan, Mike, *Sting of the Scorpion* (Sutton, 2000)

Mosley, Leonard, *The Cat and the Mice* (Arthur Barker, 1958)

Moyzisch, L.C., *Operation Cicero* (Readers Union, 1952)

Neillands, Robin, *Eighth Army* (John Murray, 2004)

Ondaatje, Michael, *The English Patient* (Bloomsbury, 1992)

Pick, Christopher, *Egypt a Traveller's Anthology* (John Murray, 1991)

Pitt, Barrie, *The Crucible of War* (Jonathan Cape, 1980)

Playfair, Major-General I.S.O., *The Mediterranean & Middle East Volume 1* (HMSO, 1954)

_____ *The Mediterranean & Middle East Volume 2* (HMSO, 1956)

_____ *The Mediterranean & Middle East Volume 3* (HMSO, 1960)

Ranfurly, Countess Hermione, *To War with Whitaker* (William Heinemann, 1994)

Sansom, A.W., *I Spied Spies* (George G. Harrap, 1965)

Sebag-Montefiore, Hugh, *Enigma* (Weidenfeld & Nicolson, 2000)

Simmons, Mark, *The Battle of Matapan 1941* (Spellmount, 2011)

Smith, Michael, *Station X The Codebreakers of Bletchley Park* (Channel 4 Books, 1998)

Stark, Freya, *Dust in the Lion's Paw* (John Murray, 1961)

Trevor-Roper, Hugh, *Herodotus* (Washington Square Press, 1963)

Whiting, Charles, *Hitler's Secret War* (Leo Cooper, 2000)

Wynter, Brigadier H.W., *Special Forces in the Desert War 1940–1943* (Public Records Office, 2001)

Young, Desmond, *Rommel the Desert Fox* (Collins, 1950)

Archives
Bletchley Park
Hungarian Geographic Museum
Imperial War Museum
Public Records Office, Kew
United States National Archives

Journals and Newspapers
Book and Magazine Collector
Daily Telegraph
National Geographic
People Magazine
Sunday Telegraph
The Times
World War II Magazine

Index